In *Rhythms of Grace*,
to experience inward
rhythms that are masked by the conflicting tempos
of a polyrhythmic world. He draws from a rich array
of personal experience and the collective wisdom of
many others to remind us of things we have forgotten,
and to inspire us to breathe afresh the life-giving grace
of God.

### Charles J. Conniry, Jr., PhD

vice president and dean, Portland Seminary at
George Fox University

author of *Soaring in the Spirit:
Rediscovering Mystery in the Christian Life*

*Rhythms of Grace* speaks to the exhaustion and burnout that many (if not most) spiritual leaders experience
sooner or later. Williams cites his own story of trying
so hard and ending up exhausted, disillusioned, and
isolated. Then with the Old Testament prophet Elijah
as a model, enormous research on the subject, and his
own pastor's heart, he takes the role of a shepherd
to the wounded. He gently leads toward rest, renewal,
and ministry realignment. Whether prevention or cure
is needed, this is a helpful book for any Christian who
feels stressed, overworked, or severely criticized.

### Charles Mylander

former superintendent of Evangelical Friends Church-
Southwest, former director of Evangelical Friends Mission

co-author with Neil Anderson of *Setting Your Church Free*

Self-care is one of the most important—yet most neglected—aspects of a sustainable, enduring pastoral ministry. So often those who dedicate their lives shepherding others toward healing and wholeness seem unsure of how to experience that same shalom in their own lives. Dave Williams's book is a spiritual roadmap for those who have lost their way. As a pastor of pastors, Dave communicates with a shepherd's heart as he guides leaders back to the Good Shepherd. Biblically-grounded, theologically astute, and enormously practical—I consider this book a must for any pastor looking to sustain or regain the unforced rhythms of life-giving grace.

### Derek Brown, PhD

professor of pastoral ministry, Barclay College

*Rhythms of Grace* is a deeply personal and practical book. With raw honesty and humble transparency, David Williams offers realistic remedies for the deadly threat of burnout. To the weary, disillusioned, and lonely, I pray that this book will encourage your soul in the profound way that it has refreshed mine.

### Fil Anderson

executive director, Journey Resources

author of *Running on Empty and Breaking the Rules*

To be human is to live rhythmically. Many of us are living painfully out of sync. It is this eternal call to rhythm that we desperately need to cure us from our ever-present sense of desperation. With Rhythms of Grace, David Williams kindly and persuasively invites us into the life that God has offered—a life of goodness and beauty; a life of rest; a rhythmic life of depth in the whirlwind of shallowness. If your life is out of sync, look no further to find the cadence that your heart has been waiting to hear.

### Curt Thompson, M.D.

founding director, Being Known

author of *Anatomy of the Soul* and *The Soul of Shame*

# Rhythms Of Grace

## Life-Saving Disciplines
## for Spiritual Leaders

David O. Williams

**BARCLAY PRESS**
Newberg, OR 97132

*Rhythms of Grace:*
*Life Saving Disciplines for Spiritual Leaders*

Barclay Press, Inc.
Newberg, Oregon
www.barclaypress.com

Cover photograph: Eric Muhr
Cover and page design: Mareesa Fawver

ISBN 9781594980404

This project is dedicated to
my fellow pastors and church leaders.

I have no higher privilege than to know you, love you,
learn from you, and partner with you in the ministry of
the gospel of our Lord Jesus Christ.

*Are you tired? Worn out? Burned out on religion? Come to me.*
*Get away with me and you'll recover your life.*
*I'll show you how to take a real rest.*
*Walk with me and work with me—*
*watch how I do it.*
*Learn the unforced rhythms of grace.*

—Matthew 11:28-29 (MSG)

# Contents

# Acknowledgments

As I pause to reflect on the process that has led to the completion of this particular project, I find myself overwhelmed by the grace and mercy of our great and mighty God. I have been immersed in his passionate, relentless, boundless love since the day I was born, but I continue to be amazed by the fresh expressions of love that he reveals to me on a regular basis. It is by the grace of our Lord Jesus Christ alone that I have been saved and set apart for service as a minister of the gospel. I humbly offer this project as a "living sacrifice," an imperfect yet heartfelt expression of my love and gratitude to God. I pray that it will be holy, pleasing, and acceptable in his sight. "May these words of my mouth and this meditation of my heart be pleasing in your sight, Lord, my Rock and my Redeemer" (Psalm 19:14). *Soli Deo Gloria!*

By his grace, the Lord has seen fit to shower me with many extraordinary gifts over the years. Next to Jesus there is none greater than the gift of my family. My parents, John and Gerry Williams, have always loved me, supported me, believed in me, and prayed for me. In fact, their encouragement served as the primary catalyst for this project. Throughout their seventy-one years of marriage and ministry together, Dad and Mom set the gold standard for faithfulness to Christ and his church. I am eternally grateful for their influence in my life.

I wasn't sure that I would ever be able to find anyone who would be able to match my parents' level of devotion to God and compassion for his people. Then the Lord introduced me to a woman named Carol. Now that we have completed over thirty years of marriage and ministry ourselves, I can say without hesitation that my parents have met their match! Without her constant encouragement and the sacrificial support of our children—Josiah and Shelby, Sarah and Gabe, Jeremiah and Wendy, Hannah and Seth, Jessie and Jasmine—I would have given up on this project a long time ago.

I also want to express my deep appreciation for the great cloud of witnesses that has surrounded me throughout this stage in my journey with Jesus. I could never have embarked on this adventure without the inspiration and encouragement of the students, faculty and administration at Barclay College. My destination is now in sight due in great part to their very tangible and unwavering support. I am also deeply grateful for my friends at Quaker Ridge Camp in Woodland Park, Colorado, who graciously provided me with an ideal setting where I could complete the bulk of my doctoral dissertation, a document that provides the conceptual framework for this book. Then there are all of my fellow doctoral students and professors from George Fox Evangelical Seminary. Each of you has made a significant contribution to my personal and professional formation, and has helped to shape the essential character and content of this project. Special thanks goes to the "Beach Fathers" (Mike, Chuck, Cranston, and Jeff), to my spiritual director, Fil Anderson, and to my dissertation advisors, Chuck Conniry and Dick Sartwell. You may not all be Quakers, but I count you all as true friends.

As I write these words, I feel compelled to recognize my personal indebtedness to the many gifted writers who have inspired me to pick up the pen and find my voice. Ironically, I wasn't much of a reader until college, where I was introduced to the writings of C. S. Lewis during the first semester of my freshman year. Lewis eventually became my all-time favorite author and through our literary association alone, I now consider "Jack" to be one of my dearest friends. In addition to Lewis, I have drawn additional inspiration from the work of Richard Foster, Dietrich Bonhoeffer, Henri Nouwen, Brennan Manning, Philip Yancey, and Eugene Peterson, among others. I am especially grateful for Peterson's translation of Matthew 11:28-29, which provides the inspiration for the title of this book.

# The Perils of Spiritual Heroism

*Elijah was afraid and ran for his life. . . . He came to a broom bush, sat down under it and prayed that he might die.*
(1 Kings 19:3-4)

## Rainy Days and Mondays

It was a cold, cloudy, mid-winter day on the north coast, typical for that time of year in northeast Ohio. I was sitting on the couch by myself in the atypically quiet living room of our home on the west side of Cleveland. Take my word for it. A family of eight, living in a small bungalow located directly below the flight path of a busy airport in a big city, is rarely quiet.

Wisely sensing that I might be in need of some personal space (my blank stares, slurred speech, and generally comatose disposition may have been a tip-off), my wife had decided to take our one-year-old twins with her to the grocery store while our four older children, ages five through twelve, were off at school. "Finally," I sighed, "a few moments of peace and quiet."

It was a normal Monday afternoon for me in many ways. Like other pastors, my biggest work day of the week was Sunday, so I had developed a habit of taking Mondays off for Sabbath rest, better known as "triage" in the world of pastoral ministry. After completing another strenuous cycle of church-related activity, it was common to feel thoroughly exhausted and even a bit melancholy on my day off, especially on this soggy winter's day in northeast Ohio. As the Carpenters once crooned, "Rainy days and Mondays always get me down."

And yet it wasn't just another typical day off from the church where I had been pastoring for the past several years. I had been feeling increasingly drained, discouraged, and defeated in my ministry at the church. We had experienced many high points during our tenure in Cleveland, to be sure. We loved the people, and they loved us. I knew I was called to be their pastor, and I felt genuinely honored to serve. But things had seemed to flatten out in recent months. No matter how hard I tried, I just couldn't seem to change things for the better. I had hit a wall.

I was at the bottom of my emotional barrel, and I couldn't deny it any longer. I had been forcing myself to maintain a consistent devotional life, hoping that a change in feelings would eventually follow on the heels of my dutiful obedience. In reality, however, I felt like I was dying on the vine. And scariest of all, especially for a pastor, for what seemed like the first time in my life, I didn't have the slightest clue how to pray.

I eventually found myself bent over, my head between my hands—grasping for words, gasping for breath. Finally, like the last remnants of moisture wrung from a well-used towel, two words slowly dripped out of my mouth, almost involuntarily: "I'm drowning."

## Rough Riders

There is no greater privilege in the Christian life than to serve as a spiritual leader within the body of Christ. As the apostle Paul testifies, "If a man is eager to be a church leader, he desires an excellent work" (1 Timothy 3:1 GNT). Those who are set apart for spiritual leadership in the body of Christ have received a high calling indeed. According to recent studies, however, they are also in for one rough ride:

- Of the 500,000 full-time, vocational pastors in the United States today, approximately one out of every four (125,000) are experiencing "burnout."
- 60 percent work more than sixty hours per week.
- 80 percent believe that ministry has adversely affected their families.
- 90 percent feel they are inadequately trained to cope with ministry demands.
- 40 percent report a serious conflict with a parishioner at least once a month.
- 37 percent confess to inappropriate sexual behavior with someone in their church (which is about the same percentage as the general population).
- 70 percent do not have someone they consider a close friend.
- 70 percent have a lower self-image than when they entered ministry.

- 70 percent say they get less than seven hours of sleep each night.
- 75 percent do not take a regular day off for Sabbath rest.
- 76 percent are overweight or obese (compared with 61 percent of the general population).
- 40 percent reported being depressed or worn out "some or most of the time."
- Not surprisingly, 40 percent of these pastors have considered leaving their ministries in the last three months alone.[1]

Needless to say, this statistical litany clearly indicates that a large proportion of our spiritual leaders currently experience an extraordinary level of job-related stress and burnout. Much as I did on that rainy Monday afternoon in mid-January, these men and women often feel as if they are drowning in a vast sea of unmet needs, unresolved conflicts, and unrealistic expectations. As a result, many of them are leaving public ministry. Many others limp along, doing their best to cope, hoping to find ways to survive with some portion of their spiritual vitality and personal integrity intact.

Like young soldiers returning from a foreign battlefield, emerging spiritual leaders are often shell shocked when they discover that the local church can be a deadly war zone as well. And far too often, it seems, we tend to shoot our wounded. Most of us know someone who fits this description. They might be serving in your church right now or, even more likely, they may have recently left. They may be your friends, or they may be part of your own family. Numbers have names, after all.

# Fallen Soldiers

All of us are familiar with the high-profile cases of prominent church leaders who have succumbed to the pitfalls and pressures of public ministry. Their names are strewn across the headlines in much the same way that the names of fallen soldiers are reported on the evening news, only with less honor.

Scandal once again rocked the church world in the fall of 2006 as allegations came to light regarding the sexual conduct of one of its most prominent evangelical leaders. Ted Haggard eventually stepped down from his position as senior pastor of the fourteen-thousand-member New Life megachurch in Colorado Springs, and as the executive director of the National Association of Evangelicals, representing more than thirty million evangelicals from across the country. In a letter written to the congregation he founded and served for over twenty years, Haggard acknowledged his immoral behavior and apologized for the damage it caused to the church and to his family:

> I am so sorry. I am sorry for the disappointment, the betrayal, and the hurt. I am sorry for the horrible example I have set for you. I have an overwhelming, all-consuming sadness in my heart for the pain that you and I and my family have experienced over the past few days. I am so sorry for the circumstances that have caused shame and embarrassment to all of you. The fact is, I am guilty of sexual immorality, and I take responsibility for the entire problem.

I am a deceiver and a liar. There is a part of my life that is so repulsive and dark that I've been warring against it all of my adult life. For extended periods of time, I would enjoy victory and rejoice in freedom. Then, from time to time, the dirt that I thought was gone would resurface, and I would find myself thinking thoughts and experiencing desires that were contrary to everything I believe and teach.

Through the years, I've sought assistance in a variety of ways, with none of them proving to be effective in me. Then, because of pride, I began deceiving those I love the most because I didn't want to hurt or disappoint them.

The public person I was wasn't a lie; it was just incomplete. When I stopped communicating about my problems, the darkness increased and finally dominated me. As a result, I did things that were contrary to everything I believe.[2]

Haggard's comments are troubling, to say the least. It is not unusual for spiritual leaders (or people from any other walk of life for that matter) to find themselves in situations where, like Ted Haggard, they end up "thinking thoughts and experiencing desires that [are] contrary to everything [they] believe and teach." What is especially revealing, though, is Haggard's confession that "I began deceiving those I love the most because I didn't want to hurt or disappoint them," and, "when I stopped communicating about my problems, the darkness increased and finally dominated me."

## Diagnosing the Disease

Case studies such as these contain within them a number of important clues that may help us to better understand the dynamics that produce such high levels of burnout and breakdown among spiritual leaders today, which so often leads to a premature departure from public ministry. But before we examine some of these core issues, we need to begin by defining the term *burnout* itself.

According to Merriam-Webster, burnout can be defined as "exhaustion of physical or emotional strength or motivation usually as a result of prolonged stress or frustration."[3] David Mann is certainly correct in his assertion that "the phenomenon of burnout was present long before Dr. Herbert Freudenberger used the phrase in 1974 to describe behaviors he observed among staff members of human service agencies."[4] Working with people has always been draining, regardless of the setting.

So how might we explain the dramatic rise in the impact of burnout among church leaders in recent years? As United Methodist clergywoman and licensed social worker Sheri Ferguson suggests, "Today's clergy seem to have greater demands and less support, and the radical changes in our society over the past 50 years have fundamentally redefined the very nature of what it means to be in ministry."[5]

This sentiment is echoed by Gwen Halaas, a family physician in Kenosha, Wisconsin, who directs the ministerial health and wellness program for the Evangelical Lutheran Church in America. According to Halaas, a major study in the 1950s began following a large cohort of clergy. The researchers found that clergy had lower rates of disease for virtually every possible diagnosis and lived longer and healthier lives than any other professional group. The results were quite different, however, when similar studies were conducted on the generations of clergy that followed. A 1983 study, for example, found that Protestant clergy had the highest overall work-related stress of various religious professionals and the next-to-lowest amount of personal resources to cope with the strain. In 1999, another study found that clergy have one of the highest death rates from heart disease of any occupation. "Basically," Halaas summarizes, "it's become a more difficult job with fewer rewards, and all those things add to stress and take a toll on health."[6]

One of the most comprehensive studies on the impact of clergy burnout was conducted several years ago as part of the Pulpit & Pew project at Duke Divinity School. Dean Hoge and Jacqueline Wenger, researchers from the Catholic University of America, were commissioned to gather new data on why so many pastors are leaving church ministry today. Respondents included nearly one thousand former leaders from five major denominations who had left local church ministry within the previous eight years.[7]

When the results were tabulated, some clear patterns emerged. According to Hoge and Wenger, "The main factors pushing local church ministers away are organizational and interpersonal. These pushes have to do with conflict, feelings of being stymied, and isolation."[8] The men and women in this study repeatedly spoke of the need to find ways to reduce the amount of stress they were experiencing. The primary source of this stress arose from conflicts with the congregation, church staff, or denominational officials. Exhausted by the constant time and energy required to manage these conflicts, leaving little time and energy to invest in the things they loved, these former leaders experienced increasing levels of dissatisfaction and disillusionment in their work. This, in turn, led to intensified feelings of loneliness and isolation, based on the fact that these leaders were in conflict with the very people who would normally serve as their primary support system (congregation, colleagues, and denominational officials).

And so the trap is set. All that is needed to spring this trap and initiate a major physical, emotional, or moral breakdown is a trigger event of some kind—a perceived failure at work, a painful crisis at home, or worse yet, a personal panic attack arising from the paralyzing fear that someone may actually find out that we are fully human after all:

> Many of us do not consider church to be a safe place to deal with basic life issues, much less our degeneracy. . . . And if you're a leader at church, the stakes are even higher. You would rather lose an index finger than undergo the disgrace of having your church find out about your sordid private life. . . . Church will only become a place of spiritual healing and transformation when we take the risk to make it the

most dangerous place of all—a place where we can be fully, completely ourselves.[9]

The practical implications of this last concern are graphically illustrated by the experience of a fellow ministry colleague who recently conveyed the following account:

When I was at [a particular church many years ago], I had to deal with major issues of depression, despair, burnout, etc. But about the time I made the decision to "do something about it" and open up to someone in the denominational structure, I was in a meeting with members of the governing board. The chairman of the board that dealt with pension and insurance issues at that time was making a report to the board about expenses related to the health insurance side of things. At one point he looked right at me, smiled, and said, "Some people have had some pretty expensive dental work done."

I smiled back and ignored his comment. But I made a mental note: *If I see a counselor about my problems it could be discussed in front of this board just like my dental repairs.* And so I resolved that if indeed I was going to see anyone, and if I didn't want that broadly known and "chatted about" I would have to make my own arrangements with a counselor without ties to the church and pay for it myself. That's what I did. My income at that time was enough that I could afford overtime to pay for that help. But many pastors are not going to have the resources to pay their own way for therapy.[10]

## Clergy in Crisis

By now it should be clear to even the most casual observer that we are in the midst of a genuine crisis in the church today. The reality is that pastors and other spiritual leaders are leaving vocational ministry faster than we can replace them. This is due primarily to the crippling effects of burnout, a pastoral pathology resulting from a lethal combination of extraordinary job-related stress and woefully inadequate self-care. As we have seen, this disturbing trend has devastating implications not only for church leaders and their families, but for the body of Christ as a whole: "If one part suffers, every part suffers with it" (1 Corinthians 12:26). The church cannot "[build] itself up in love [unless] each part does its work" (Ephesians 4:16), and this requires the ministry of equipping that has been uniquely entrusted to church leaders (Ephesians 4:11-12).

It might also be useful to note that the Chinese word for *crisis* is actually derived from a character that combines two symbols, one representing *despair* and the other representing *opportunity*.[11] This reminds us that whenever we face a crisis of any kind, regardless of whether it was forced upon us or self-inflicted, we have crucial choices to make. How we respond to a given crisis will have lasting consequences for us and for all those we influence.

## Elijah and the Perils of Spiritual Heroism

While the challenges facing church leaders today are considerable, they are by no means unique to this

25

generation. Spiritual leaders throughout biblical history have faced similar, if not greater obstacles, and they all had critical choices to make along the way as well. Moses grew so weary from leading the Israelites (or was it the "Grumblites"?), for example, that he literally wanted to die (Numbers 11:10-15). David was forced to run for his life in order to escape Saul's envy-driven death threats (1 Samuel 22:1-2). Jeremiah became so disgusted with the whole prophetic enterprise that he resorted to accusing God of outright deception (Jeremiah 20:7). Jonah's disillusionment with God's providential plan caused him to develop a chip on his shoulder the size of a small nation and, like Moses, he found himself yearning for annihilation (Jonah 4). Not to be outdone by his predecessors, Peter was so overwhelmed by his own failure to follow the call of Christ at one point that he could find no other alternative than to give up public ministry altogether and return to his previous occupation in the fishing industry (John 21). Thankfully, there was much more to each of these leaders' stories, but the episodes highlighted here should more than prove the point. Ministry is hard—always has been, always will be.

While each of the examples has much to offer when it comes to understanding the dynamics of burnout among spiritual leaders, the prophet Elijah's experience is especially intriguing in this regard. As previously noted, research has shown that there is a common pattern that precipitates nearly every case of clergy burnout: exhaustion → disillusionment → isolation → breakdown. When we review the biblical record in light of this information, it is not hard to see why Elijah, one of the greatest leaders in the history of God's people, found himself preferring death over continued ministry (1 Kings 19:4).

Throughout his first few years of ministry preceding the breakdown at Mt. Horeb, Elijah worked tirelessly to stem the tide of paganism in Israel, which had become increasingly rampant under the fraudulent leadership of King Ahab and his infamous wife, Queen Jezebel. This ongoing conflict finally came to a head at Mt. Carmel where Elijah summoned the people to gather, along with Ahab and all 850 of Jezebel's pagan prophets. Once everyone had assembled, the prophet summarized the situation succinctly: "How long will you waver between two opinions? If the LORD is God, follow him; but if Baal is God, follow him" (1 Kings 18:21). Hearing no response, Elijah decided to up the ante by challenging the prophets of Baal to a spiritual duel of sorts. Despite the fact that the odds were 850:1, Elijah's prophetic authority was confirmed with unmistakable clarity that day, as was Yahweh's unparalleled supremacy. When the people of Israel recognized this, every shred of ambiguity suddenly disappeared as they fell down and cried out with one voice: "Yahweh is God! Yahweh is God!" (1 Kings 18:39 NJB).

This was heady stuff for a relatively inexperienced leader like Elijah. It might also be useful to remember at this point that Elijah's name in Hebrew is literally translated, "Yahweh is God." This raises some interesting questions. Were the people crying out to the Lord their God with newfound loyalty and allegiance that day on the slopes of Mt. Carmel, or were they expressing their adulation for the prophet who happened to be presiding over this whole affair? And what was Elijah thinking? Were his motives so pure that he was immune to any temptation towards self-aggrandizement, or is it possible that he found himself taking a little too much pleasure in the fact that thousands of people were bowing down before him, shouting his name in impassioned unison? If what follows this episode is any indication, it would appear that the latter scenario may be more accurate than we would like to think. It may also be more liberating.

At some place in the heart of every spiritual leader, there is a longing to be the spiritual hero. Like Neo in *The Matrix*, we all want to be "the One" on whom people can count, to be indispensable. Ironically, perhaps the most dangerous moment for a spiritual leader is when he or she actually gets to taste it. Elijah certainly did. And it almost killed him.

It takes a lot of energy to be a hero. In fact, it is downright exhausting. Human beings are not well-suited to play the role of Messiah. None of us is remotely qualified for the job. But as Donald Hands and Wayne Fehr have learned from their many years of counseling experience with church leaders, most of us will try our very best to fake it:

> The hero is almost a given role, near axiom-atic, even archetypal, for clergy. The hero fixes others, achieves status in the community, and focuses energies and affect on the prob-lems of others. The hero works long hours,

skips vacations, or if on vacation is bored and restless. The hero is well trained to run away from the emptiness or loneliness that might be uncovered during "time off"; it is better to keep working. This culminates in the "Messiah complex," the hero's delusion that his or her efforts are both supremely ordained and indispensable for others' health and salvation.[12]

Spiritual heroism is lethal because it is just one step away from idolatry, the very thing that Elijah so adamantly opposed throughout his life and ministry. In reality, it is simply a more subtle form of the satanic whisper that began this whole downward spiral toward death and destruction in our world. "You will be like God," the serpent hissed (Genesis 3:5). This must have sounded especially attractive to Elijah at Mt. Carmel. It had his name written all over it.

Satan tried this one on Jesus, too, during his temptation in the wilderness. But Jesus would have none of it. As Henri Nouwen reminds us, even the Messiah did not have a "Messiah complex":

> The second temptation to which Jesus was exposed was precisely the temptation to do something spectacular, something that could win him great applause. "Throw yourself down from the temple and let the angels catch you and carry you in their arms" (Matthew 4:6). But Jesus refused to be a stunt man. He did not come to prove himself. He did not come to walk on hot coals, swallow fire, or put his hand in the lion's mouth to demonstrate that he had something worthwhile to say.[13]

Spiritual heroism is the disease that lies at the core of clergy burnout. Like HIV, it may remain dormant for a time, but if left untreated, the symptoms will eventually manifest themselves. Spiritual heroism inevitably leads to exhaustion, because it requires enormous amounts of energy to play God. It inevitably leads to disillusionment, because it is impossible to keep up the charade indefinitely. And it inevitably leads to isolation, because, when you are "God," it is really hard to find another human being who is your equal.

As Sally Morgenthaler can testify, spiritual heroism also fuels addictive behavior and other forms of moral meltdown that accompany the disease because it requires the leader to invest an enormous amount of energy in the self-defeating practice of "image management." This helps to explain how high profile leaders like Ted Haggard, or Sally's own husband, can suddenly crash and burn:

> Many pastors paint unrealistic pictures of themselves. This kind of leader carefully crafts a leadership icon, rather than presenting his God-given, multi-faceted self. This kind of leader sets himself up for failure.
>
> Image building is a dangerous game. And it's at the core of addictive behavior. . . . If a pastor comes into the ministry with an addictive family background or has otherwise developed addictive tendencies, a congregational system that requires him to uphold an impossible, squeaky-clean image is going to function like a match to the gasoline.

Whenever pastors try to hide behind this patina, the chances of latent addictive behavior escalating is extremely high. The more impossibly perfect the pastoral image, the greater the need to engage in taboo behavior.[14]

## The Remedy for Spiritual Heroism

So what is the cure for spiritual heroism? It is the same course of action that Elijah and every other true prophet of the Lord would prescribe for behavior that is contrary to the revealed will of God: repentance. We must turn from the error and futility of our ways, receive God's gracious promise of forgiveness, and allow God to restore to us the joy of our salvation (See Psalm 51:12). As the psalmist learned from personal experience, we must realize that blessing comes through brokenness.[15] But we can also rejoice in the reality that a broken spirit is the best safeguard against the more devastating and potentially fatal effects of a full-blown physical, emotional, moral, or spiritual meltdown.

Pastor Peter Scazzero speaks from personal experience when he argues that the fruit of repentance for spiritual leaders must include a willingness to receive the gift of limits:

> Understanding and respecting our boundaries and limits is one of the most important character qualities and skills leaders need in order to be long-term lovers of God and others. . . . The frightening truth is that we can sometimes pass through our God-given limits and end up doing God's work without God!

Understanding the gift of limits enables us to affirm self-care. It is one of the greatest challenges for those who serve others. As Parker Palmer says, "Self-care is never a selfish act—it is simply good stewardship of the only gift I have, the gift I was put on earth to offer to others. Anytime we can listen to true self and give it the care it requires, we do so not only for ourselves, but for the many others whose lives we touch."[16]

If there was one thing that Elijah gained during his encounter with God at Mt. Horeb, it was a renewed willingness to receive the gift of limits; and embracing these limits literally saved his life. Based on 1 Kings 19, a biblical plan for preventing and/or treating burnout might include the following course of action:

- Physical refreshment: a remedy for exhaustion (1 Kings 19:5-8)
- Spiritual renewal: a remedy for disillusionment (1 Kings 19:9-14)
- Vocational realignment: a remedy for isolation (1 Kings 19:15-21)

As we will see in the pages that follow, when practiced on a regular basis, these "renewing rituals"[17] or "rhythms of grace"[18] prove to be lifesaving disciplines for spiritual leaders, capable of strengthening our immune systems against the onslaught of the core disease that lies behind the multifaceted symptoms of clergy burnout—spiritual heroism. The very fact that we need them reminds us that we do have limits; in other words—we are not God.

## Making it Personal

1.  On a scale from 1 to 10 (10 being high), how would you rate the current level of stress in your life?

2.  As you reflect on some of the statistics regarding the current state of church leadership, are there any areas of concern that you can relate to personally?

3.  Are you aware of any core needs in your life that are not being adequately addressed?

4.  If a building inspector were to examine the foundations of your personal life (the part that is below the surface and that no one else can see) what might they find?

# Chapter One

## The Rhythm of Physical Refreshment: A Remedy for Exhaustion

*Get up and eat, for the journey is too much for you.*
(1 Kings 19:7)

### The Sacrament of the Sweaty Towel

When I close my eyes, I can still smell the sweet aroma. Depending on the day or the occasion, it may have been the smell of fresh bread baking in the oven or a juicy pot roast greeting us on our return from church. Perhaps most memorable of all, there was the annual Thanksgiving feast, complete with turkey, dressing, cranberry sauce, pumpkin pie, and all the fixings. At our house, family meals were a bonafide sacrament—messy yet mysteriously holy moments when we all encountered the tangible, incarnational presence of God in our midst.

Behind the endless array of scrumptious food that we shared together, there was always one woman: my mother. Like so many great cooks before her who practiced their trade for the glory of God, Gerry Williams's kitchen was her prayer closet, and the dining room was her mission field. If you asked those who watched her work, they would be quick to tell you that Mom wasn't merely cooking. Like Brother Lawrence, her monastic forebear, she was "practicing the presence of God." When she was engaged in the ministry of cooking, she did so with a feverish combination of unbridled joy and unparalleled passion. So much so that she almost always wore a sweaty towel around her neck.

Through her faithful stewardship of God's gift of hospitality, or "the sacrament of the sweaty towel," I think it is safe to say that Mom probably blessed more people in Jesus' name than most preachers will ever be able to touch from a church pulpit. During her ninety-four years on planet earth, Mom prepared countless meals for her husband and seven children, as well as her twenty-five grandchildren, twenty-nine great-grandchildren, more than sixty foster children, and an endless number of church members, college students, friends, neighbors, co-workers, and complete strangers. For Mom, cooking was much more than a domestic duty. It was a sacred act of Christian service, her "living sacrifice" to our good and gracious God, the heavenly founder of every human feast.

Mom was far from perfect, of course. She was a frail, finite, fallen human being, just like the rest of us, a sinner saved by the grace of God alone. But make no mistake about it. God's grace had a dramatically transformational effect upon Mom's life. The passionate, relentless, unconditional love of God compelled her to love others in like manner.

"Freely you have received," Jesus said, "freely give" (Matthew 10:8). Long before Brennan Manning penned the words, Mom boldly proclaimed the truth that "God loves us as we are, not as we should be." And with remarkable consistency, she practiced what she preached.

By surrendering her life to the unconditional love of God, Mom was empowered by the Holy Spirit to become a living icon of our Lord Jesus Christ. As a flawed yet faithful *theotokos* or God-bearer, her life bore an unusually authentic witness to the gospel. Mom had discovered the secret that greatness is not found in doing great things for God, but in doing small things with great love.

When I get to heaven, I have no doubt that the first person to greet me will be Jesus. Based on her gift of hospitality, my guess is that my mom will probably be second in line. She will welcome me with a big hug and a warm smile, as usual. And when we are invited to take our seats at the great heavenly banquet table, I won't be a bit surprised to look over and see my mom wearing a sweaty towel around her neck.

## First Things First

To the best of my knowledge, there is no biblical evidence to suggest that angels perspire. But in my mind's eye, I can easily imagine a sweaty towel draped around the neck of the cherub that was chosen to provide much-needed sustenance for a much-beleaguered prophet during his solitary sojourn through the Judean wilderness. After all, angels are given some of the most important and, it would appear, some of the most demanding tasks to perform in God's great kingdom. What greater and more strenuous ministry could an angel have than to serve as the primary instrument of physical rejuvenation for Elijah, one of the greatest prophets to ever walk the face of the earth? If you're old enough to remember, try picturing Angelo Dundee in Muhammad Ali's corner of the ring during the fifteenth round of a Frazier fight, then ratchet it up about a million times or so.

But I digress.

Let's pick up the story again in 1 Kings 19. Following his courageous confrontation with King Ahab and the prophets of Baal at Mt. Carmel—which had to be one of the most exhilarating and exhausting ministry assignments in human history—Elijah found himself running for his life, even wanting to die (1 Kings 19:3-4). This unexpected turn of events almost takes your breath away as you follow the story. The fearless prophet, previously confident and seemingly invincible, suddenly appears to panic, fleeing for his life. Elijah was scared to death!

What in the world happened? How does a mighty man of God abruptly turn into a paranoid, depressed, suicidal basket case?

The answer is actually quite simple. Elijah was *homoiopathes* (James 5:17). He was "a man with a nature like ours" (ESV), "as completely human as we are" (TLB), "a man subject to like passions as we are" (KJV). In other words, Elijah was an ordinary human being, "just as we are" (NIRV).

If we take the time to pay close attention to the Lord's response to Elijah in the midst of this crisis, some of us may be somewhat surprised to find that that he was not the least bit upset with Elijah over his sudden failure of nerve. Unlike so many of us, God does not scold or berate his children in the midst of their brokenness. "As a father has compassion on his children," the psalmist reminds us, "so the LORD has compassion on those who fear him; for he knows how we are formed, he remembers that we are dust" (Psalm 103:13-14).

Because of God's intimate knowledge of Elijah's humanity and his deep concern for the welfare of his own child, we really should not be surprised to find that the first three things the Lord prescribed for Elijah as a remedy for his condition were the following: a good meal, a good night's sleep, and a good workout (1 Kings 19:5-8).

Doesn't sound very spiritual, does it? Let's be honest. As seminary-trained church leaders, most of us would have readily admonished Elijah to read a particular passage of Scripture or pray a particular type of prayer as the first step in his recovery process. Most of us have been conditioned to believe that the answer to almost every challenge we face in life is a spiritual one. In one sense this may be true, but only when we are willing to expand our definition of the word *spirituality*. Elijah's story reminds us that sometimes the most spiritual things we can do are eat, sleep and exercise. As followers of Jesus Christ, the incarnate Son of God, the Word made flesh (John 1:14), we of all people should understand. We follow an eating, sleeping, exercising Savior. We are embodied spirits, after all.

As a Christian psychiatrist, Curt Thompson takes this connection between the body and the soul very seriously. He spent years studying the relationship between Christian spirituality and interpersonal neuroscience in an effort to offer genuine hope and healing to the broken people he meets on a daily basis. In his book, *Anatomy of the Soul*, Thompson reminds us of the need to recognize the critical interplay between the life of the soul (or mind) and the life of the body:

> The mind is embodied, which means that it is housed in your physical self and depends on your body to function. . . . As Christians, we sometimes dismiss our physical experience as inferior to the abstract, ethereal part of our consciousness where we "imagine" or "think about" spiritual matters. Yet Paul describes our bodies as temples of the Holy Spirit, so clearly they're involved in our deepest spiritual experiences. In fact, in order to love God with your mind you must love him with your body. If you are not paying attention to what your body (or "gut") is telling you, it will be difficult to love God with your mind because you will be disconnected from it.[19]

Thankfully, when the angel of the Lord found Elijah sprawled beneath a broom tree in the middle of the desert, he didn't hand him a Bible. Elijah wouldn't have had enough strength to pick it up (even if one would have been available at the time). Without question, the time would come when the sleepy seer would need a fresh revelation from God. But at that moment he was completely and thoroughly exhausted. He had just come through what had to be the most traumatic experience in his entire life to that point. Humanly speaking, there is no way he should have survived.

Following a supernatural sprint from Mt. Carmel to Jezreel (twenty-five miles) and his panic-stricken flight from Jezreel to Beersheba (one hundred miles), Elijah set off on yet another strenuous hike, traveling "a day's journey" (fifteen miles) into the desert. After an expedition like this, apparently without any food or water, Elijah was in desperate need of physical refreshment. It was only after he had received this gift of physical renewal, generously administered by an angel of the Lord, that he was able to experience the additional blessings of spiritual and vocational renewal as well. God had to get Elijah's body right before he could speak to his spirit.

## Honoring the Body

Everywhere we go these days we are being reminded of the importance of physical fitness. The personal health benefits of eating right, sleeping well, and exercising regularly have been well documented in recent years. Anyone who hopes to "live long and prosper," as Mr. Spock was apt to say, will surely recognize the value of these disciplines and make them a central part of their daily lives. As disciples of Jesus, this takes on even greater significance when we remember that our bodies have now become temples of the Holy Spirit

(1 Corinthians 3:16). We are called to be good stewards of these bodies on loan from God.

Stephanie Paulsell, a visiting lecturer at Harvard Divinity School and author of *Honoring the Body*, offers this summary:

> For Christians, health and wellness are not just "physical" issues, but are deeply rooted theological concerns that, rightly understood, will require a change in thinking[20] about the body. . . . Everything in the Gospel [including the Incarnation itself] . . . suggests that bodies matter to God, and through our bodies we're invited to be in deep relationship with God.
>
> People need to understand that ministry isn't done by the disembodied mind, but by the whole embodied self. . . . We need churches to be communities where we talk about bodies and the care of bodies and what God expects from us.[21]

Studies of pastors and church leaders have repeatedly demonstrated clear connections between our level of physical fitness and our capacity for effective, long-term kingdom impact.[22] Unfortunately, this is an area of neglect among most clergy. As indicated earlier in this document, the majority of pastors are either overweight or obese, they get less than seven hours of sleep each night, and most do not have a regularly scheduled and implemented exercise routine. It is not surprising then, that clergy have one of the highest death rates from heart disease of any occupation.[23]

Archibald Hart, former dean of the School of

Psychology at Fuller Seminary, is one of many experts who emphasize the necessity of adequate self-care, especially for those who spend the majority of their time caring for others. In his book, *Adrenaline and Stress*, Hart helps us connect the dots between spiritual heroism, inadequate self-care, and the crippling effects of burnout, such as heart disease:

> Most of us live in a highly competitive and demanding life situation . . . constantly on the move, striving to outdo others as we reach for greater things. In fact, most of us live our whole lives in what is essentially a constant state of emergency and hurry. We become dependent on the overproduction of adrenaline, not simply for our accomplishments, but just to survive each day. The problem with our dependence on high levels of adrenaline is that we have to pay the piper for this abuse later on. What it amounts to is accelerated "wear and tear" on our cardiovascular systems, creating burnout—much like a high performance car that has been allowed to overheat.[24]

Part of the solution, Hart suggests, is to develop better eating habits, including a reduction in the intake of saturated fats and high cholesterol foods. But his central argument throughout this particular book is that we have to look beyond the menu and find ways to change our basic pace of life. According to Hart, we are a nation (and a church) that has become addicted to adrenaline. Some of the symptoms of this adrenaline addiction include intense depression, difficulty getting energy going, being overcome by great tiredness, exhaustion and feelings of panic (sound familiar, Elijah?). Hart goes on to suggest that we can learn to manage stress and control our adrenaline levels by practicing effective relaxation, improving our sleeping habits, and paying attention to our own spiritual development.[25]

"This is not a call for guilt trips," declares Lloyd Rediger, "it is a wakeup call for those of us who have accepted the privilege of spiritual leadership." The author of *Clergy Killers* goes on to emphasize the need for physical fitness among spiritual leaders as "responsible stewardship" and a primary resource for coping with conflict and spiritual attack in ministry. "When we are physically fit," Rediger continues, "we experience less pain, we are less vulnerable, and we have more endurance and flexibility."[26]

According to the God of the Bible, then, the One who formed Elijah and every other person on this planet in his own image, the One who knows us better than we know ourselves, three of the most critical disciplines related to self-care that we can and should practice if we hope to survive the enormous challenges and constant stress of public ministry are: eating right, sleeping well and exercising regularly.

## Eating Right

If there is a downside to growing up in a family where meals are considered a sacrament, it is the inherent temptation to overindulge. Feasting is a good, beautiful, and thoroughly biblical practice, but gluttony is her ugly cousin. Because good food is such a source of godly pleasure, it is easy to wind up worshiping the gift instead of the Giver.

Ironically, this tends to be an even bigger struggle for those of us in church leadership. Two words should suffice: church potluck. Can I get a witness?

For many of us, the problem is only exacerbated when we find ourselves experiencing an unusually high level of stress or conflict—which is pretty much all of the time. It's not hard to understand how this can quickly become a recipe for disaster. Overindulging in our favorite comfort food is a way to numb the pain for a while. Before we know it, a blessed sacrament can quickly degenerate into a destructive and potentially life-threatening addiction.[27]

According to Paulsell, we must encourage spiritual leaders to practice a way of eating that "draws deeply on Christian faith" and is shaped by "choices that honor the body—our body and the bodies of others."[28] While cautioning against an unhealthy preoccupation with food, Paulsell does offer a number of practical suggestions, such as fasting from junk food, eating less meat, taking care not to waste food, and never eating without saying thanks. These are small but important steps, she asserts, that can help us remember that food is a gift from God.

## Sleeping Well

In a recent survey conducted by the Barna Research Group, Americans were asked what they most looked forward to in life. "Getting a good night of sleep" was chosen by seven out of ten adults (71 percent), far and away the most popular response. This should not be surprising, considering the fact that as many as 50 million Americans sleep poorly, with one in five suffering from "stress-related insomnia,"[29] not to mention the increasing prevalence of sleep apnea and other sleeping disorders. In summarizing the results of the Barna survey, the directors observed, "The fact that millions of Americans dream about having a good night of sleep is indicative of the lifestyle people lead. . . . We voluntarily exhaust ourselves and then wonder why life doesn't seem satisfying."[30]

Archibald Hart would remind us that, as adrenaline junkies, our sleeplessness is directly related to our hyper-arousal throughout the day. We may even become convinced that getting too much sleep is a sign of laziness, weakness, or a lack of spiritual zeal. The truth, Hart retorts, is that we need all the sleep we can get. He goes on to cite the work of experts at the National Commission on Sleep Disorders, who recommend that the average person get a minimum of seven to eight hours of sleep each night. Based on his experience, Hart actually believes this is on the low end, and strongly suggests that a good stress-prevention plan would include between eight and ten hours of sleep each night, with an average of nine. Some people may need as much as eleven hours, he adds, depending on their age, lifestyle, and level of physical health. The bottom line, Hart concludes, is that "most of us could improve our physical and emotional health dramatically if we just slept or rested a little longer than usual."[31]

For those who find it unusually difficult to fall asleep or develop consistent sleep patterns, it may be helpful to experiment with a few simple practices. For example, try to go to bed at the same time every night. Prepare for bedtime by giving your body time to wind down or decompress (reading, warm bath, disconnecting from all electronics). Consider an occasional power nap during the day (twenty to thirty minutes), especially before or after periods of unusually high stress.[32] If none of these techniques help, it may be time to consult a medical professional.

## Exercising Regularly

Thanks to advances in modern technology and a seemingly insatiable appetite for materialistic comfort, Americans have become some of the most sedentary people on the planet. Although our ethnocentricity often blinds us to this reality, the blinders quickly come off when we have opportunities to interact with foreign missionaries during their time at home on furlough. Upon their return to the United States, one of the first things our cross-cultural missionaries have repeatedly spoken of in recent years is their amazement at the dramatic increase in the size of our big-screen television monitors and overstuffed chairs. The most highly toned muscle in many American bodies today may be the one attached to whichever thumb happens to be operating the remote control.

As indicated earlier, spiritual leaders are not immune from this couch-potato mentality, with fifty-seven percent of pastors stating that they do not have a regularly scheduled and implemented exercise routine.[33] This only exacerbates health concerns arising from poor nutrition and insufficient sleep. When combined with the extraordinarily high levels of stress that normally accompany church leadership, it is easy to see how this can quickly become a lethal combination.

The good news is that it does not require a personal trainer or an expensive membership in a local health club to make the necessary adjustments in this area of self-care. Most health experts suggest that it only requires thirty minutes of exercise per day, five days per week to maintain an adequate level of physical fitness. Most importantly, this can incorporate low impact exercise, such as brisk walking, hiking, or cycling. While full-court basketball may no longer be a viable option for many of us, I can testify from personal experience that there is nothing like a good bike ride to get the blood pumping, relieve stress, and burn off a few extra calories.

The most critical factor in any fitness program—whether it involves eating, sleeping, or exercising—is not primarily the level of physical effort involved, but the integrity and intentionality with which we approach these personal disciplines. These are core characteristics of what Sam Rima refers to as "the art of self-leadership":

> What allows a leader to develop an organization that is healthy and vibrant, while the leader himself is grossly overweight and struggles with his own personal health and fitness? . . . It is time that leaders, particularly spiritual leaders, begin to master the art of self-leadership to the same degree that they

have mastered and practiced the techniques of organizational leadership. If a leader's life does not reflect the same degree of excellence and skill that is manifested in the organization to which she gives leadership, it will eventually result in a dissonance that will erode the trust and respect of those being led. In today's environment, where significant leadership failures are frequent in virtually every arena and there exists a pervasive cynicism and lack of trust directed toward those in leadership, mastering the art of self-leadership has never been more essential to the achievement of effective, holistic leadership.[34]

## Making it Personal

1. In which of these three areas (eating right, sleeping well, exercising regularly) are you experiencing the most blessing?

2. In which of these three areas are you experiencing the greatest struggle?

3. Can you identify any issues that may contribute to this area of difficulty?

4. By God's grace, what practical steps can you take to improve or sustain your own health and physical fitness today?

# Chapter Two

## The Rhythm of Spiritual Renewal:
## A Remedy for Disillusionment

*Go out and stand on the mountain in the presence of the*
Lord. (1 Kings 19:11)

### The Discipline of the Empty Chair

As I write these words, I am gazing at one of my favorite images. It is a photograph I took a few years ago while hiking around Sprague Lake, a pristine mountain oasis located at the south end of Rocky Mountain National Park. At the center of this picture there is an alpine lake, surrounded by a vast forest of Douglas fir and ponderosa pine. Enthroned in the background are the majestic, snow-capped summits that preside over this portion of the Continental Divide: Flattop, Thatchtop, Chief's Head, Long's Peak. In the foreground, at the bottom of the photograph, there is an empty bench made of rough, hand-hewn timber that has my name on it, or so it would seem. As naturalist John Muir was known to say, "The mountains are calling and I must go."

This is the image that greets me nearly every morning as I open my laptop and begin another day of work. As an avid hiker and mountaineer, it reminds me to give thanks for the breath-taking beauty I have been privileged to behold, while stirring within me a fresh hunger for exploring the multitude of new destinations that are just waiting to be discovered. More importantly, as a disciple of Jesus Christ, the empty bench serves as a regular reminder that our risen Lord is inviting me to recognize his presence, to engage him in conversation, to join him on the journey, and to allow him to be the strength of my life at every point along the way: "I lift my eyes to the mountains—where does my help come from? My help comes from the LORD, the Maker of heaven and earth" (Psalm 121:1-2).[1]

This is easier said than done, of course. Like everyone else, I too have an endless number of competing voices pulling at me from every direction from morning until night, both internally and externally. And I want very much to respond to them, to please them, or to appease them at the very least. I want to have a sense that I am valued, appreciated, affirmed, loved.

But among the many capricious voices clamoring for my attention, there is but one Voice that has the ability to satisfy the deepest longings of my heart. Augustine was right: "Our hearts are restless until they rest in You, O Lord."[2] At the end of the day, we ultimately live, move, and have our being before an audience of one.

This became unusually clear to me during my first weeks on the job at Barclay College, a small Bible college located on the wind-blown prairie of south central Kansas. I moved to the sunflower state by myself in August 2000, leaving my wife and six children in Ohio, waiting for our house to sell. Although I was extremely excited to begin my new adventure on the college campus, I was less than thrilled to do it by myself. I was the new kid on the block, living alone in an empty house, occasionally feeling like I was stranded on a desert island in the middle of a tiny, remote village in the middle of—somewhere.

I'd endured two or three weeks of this solitary confinement, when the Lord decided it was time to crash my little pity party. As usual, he did so in a very kind and unexpected manner. As I was laying down for bed one night, I noticed something that had been there all along. It was there when I sat down for dinner, it was there when I rode in the car, it was there when I flew on the plane, and it was there when I was at work in my office.

"It" was an empty chair. Except that it wasn't empty. The Lord was gently reminding me that what appeared to be an empty chair was, in a very real sense, continually occupied by the One who promised to be with me "always, to the very end of the age" (Matthew 28:20). He was with me when I laid my head on the pillow each night, when I got into the car each morning, when I took my seat on the plane, and when I sat down to work on each and every course syllabus. He was with me, and he wasn't going anywhere. He was just hoping that I would notice.

As this simple reality began to sink in, the Lord began to transform my loneliness into a whole new appreciation for solitude. It wasn't long before the silence became increasingly welcome as a personal invitation to engage in intimate, uninterrupted conversation and ongoing companionship with Christ. As Paul Tillich said, "Loneliness is a word to describe the pain of being alone; solitude is a word to describe the glory of being alone."

In time, the house in Ohio sold, and my family was finally able to join me in Kansas. As thankful as I was to have them all with me, I was somewhat disappointed to discover that it was suddenly much harder to find an empty chair. But the lesson was not wasted. I have learned to practice the discipline of the empty chair. To this day, when I find an empty chair next to me along the way, I am reminded that it is not empty. The Lord is with me, and he's not going anywhere. He is my constant companion and friend. He is just waiting for me to acknowledge his presence, to engage him in conversation, to join him on the journey. And when I do, my spirit sings for joy:

> And He walks with me, and He talks with me,
> And He tells me I am his own;
> And the joy we share as we tarry there,
> None other has ever known.[3]

## Frantic Fidelity

So why do we find it so hard to simply sit still and wait upon the Lord? Quaker author Thomas Kelly summarized our situation quite well:

> The problem we face today needs very little time for its statement. Our lives . . . grow too complex and overcrowded. . . . In frantic fidelity we try to meet at least the necessary minimum of calls upon us. But we're weary and breathless. And we know and regret that our life is slipping away. . . . In guilty regret we must postpone till next week that deeper life of unshaken composure in the holy Presence, where we sincerely know our true home is, for this week is much too full.[4]

For those of us who serve in Christian leadership, words like these can strike us in much the same way that a prize fighter might land a blow to the gut of his opponent. The truth hurts. And it hurts even more when we have been hit in the same place many times before. We feel vulnerable. Our weak spot has been exposed.

We are all familiar with "frantic fidelity." We live in a time of unprecedented complexity and confusion. Our emerging iCulture (iPods, iPads, iTunes, iPhones) is obsessed with novelties, gadgets and an endless variety of time-saving electronic devices (the last time I checked, there were over a million apps available for the iPhone alone!).

According to recent studies, the average time that adults in the United States currently spend with all major media (online, mobile, television, video, radio, etc.) was a whopping twelve hours per day (nearly one half of the day or two thirds of waking hours).[5] If a similar survey was conducted among children under the age of eighteen, the numbers would undoubtedly be much higher. The world has never known a society with more leisure time on its hands, and yet we are among the most chronically exhausted, stressed-out people on the planet.

In his book *Testament of Devotion*, Kelly provides us with an eerily Elijah-esque description of our common condition as well as our common cry:

> We are not integrated. We are distraught. We feel honestly the pull of many obligations and try to fulfill them all. And we are unhappy, uneasy, strained, oppressed, and fearful we shall be shallow. For over the margins of life comes a whisper, a faint call, a premonition of richer living which we know we are passing by. Strained by the very mad pace of our daily outer burdens, we are further strained by an inward uneasiness, because we have hints that there is a way of life vastly richer and deeper than all this hurried existence, a life of unhurried serenity and peace and power. If only we could slip over into that Center! If only we could find the Silence which is the source of Sound![6]

Thankfully, there is hope for those of us who continue to struggle against the forces that would keep us from "slipping over into that Center" of divine love, out of which we are enabled to love others as we have been loved by God. This hope can be found not only in the words that spiritual leaders like Thomas Kelly have written, but in the lives they have lived. For Kelly, living out of the Divine Center came late in life, with the pivotal event taking place sometime in the autumn of 1937. According to the author's friend and biographer, Douglas Steere, it was during this time that "a new life direction took place in Thomas Kelly. No one knows exactly what happened, but . . . a fissure in him seemed to close, cliffs caved in and filled up a chasm, and what was divided grew together within him." A year later, following a summer visit among Friends in Germany, Kelly himself testified to Steere, "It is wonderful. I have been literally melted down by the love of God."[7]

Could it be that each of us is not so different from Thomas Kelly, not to mention every other spiritual leader who has gone before us? Could it be that the quickest way to the Divine Center is to recognize and renounce our tendency to live on the fringe of God's purpose for our lives? Could it be that the only way for the spiritual fissures in our lives to close is by allowing the retaining walls we have built up around our souls to cave in? Could it be that the best antidote for "frantic fidelity" is a "holy meltdown"?

Like Elijah, God is calling each of us to remember that it is his work, not ours, of which we are invited to be a part. "It is not we alone who are at work in the world, frantically finishing a work to be offered to God," Thomas Kelly summarizes, so "we need not get frantic. He is at the helm. And when our little day is done we lie down quietly in peace, for all is well."[8]

## A Slippery Slope

The pursuit of spiritual heroism not only leads to exhaustion, but it inevitably generates an overwhelming sense of disillusionment in the process. This was certainly the case for Elijah following his dramatic encounter with the prophets of Baal at Mt. Carmel. He had done everything he possibly could to expose the futility of the Phoenician fertility cult. When such efforts failed to persuade Ahab and the people of Israel to forsake these pagan gods and return fully to the Lord, the gloves came off and Yahweh himself made a point to confirm the prophet's message with unmistakable clarity. There was only one problem—it didn't work. Or at least not the way Elijah was hoping and expecting that it would.

Imagine the initial exhilaration this triumphant prophet must have been feeling as he was leading the royal chariot all the way back to Jezreel in an apparent victory parade. Adrenaline must have been rushing through every part of his body as he imagined the joyous welcome that was surely awaiting him when he arrived at his destination. Accompanied by a surprisingly cooperative king and the return of much-needed rain to the parched Palestinian countryside, Elijah must have anxiously anticipated the moment when the evil Queen Jezebel herself would finally be forced to acknowledge Yahweh's supremacy, bowing before his designated prophet as an expression of her unqualified surrender. He could hardly wait!

What a crushing disappointment it must have been when Elijah was greeted upon his arrival at Jezreel, not with shouts of acclamation but with wanted posters and death threats circulating throughout the city. Yahweh's demonstration of power at Mt. Carmel had left the prophet's archrival anything but subdued and submissive. Jezebel wanted Elijah's head on a platter. This unexpected turn of events left the seemingly invincible prophet overcome by fear, to be sure, but a much deeper and more devastating sensation was lurking just below the surface, and it was about to erupt:

> Fear is hardly all there is to say about Elijah's reaction when learning of Jezebel's outrage. . . . Profound disillusionment presents itself as another possible view of Elijah's state of mind. . . . The success at Mount Carmel leads him to expect that the fallacy of Baal worship has been exposed and his opponents definitively subdued. However, the results fall short of his expectations, as evidenced by Jezebel's unyielding antagonism. . . . When Elijah tries to come to grips with the failure of the crushing display of power to soften his antagonist, he retreats dejected to Horeb. . . . If fear is the emotion that starts him off on the long journey, it is not what motivates him to complete it.[9]

This also helps to explain why Elijah not only ran from Jezebel, but ran directly to Mt. Horeb. There were any number of other places, most of them much less distant, where he could have gone to escape from the queen's fury and recover his physical strength if that was all he had lost. But the fact that he chose Horeb as his specific destination indicates that he was looking for more than physical safety and security. Elijah was in desperate search of a way to make sense of what he had just experienced. It was not so much his fear of Jezebel that drove him to Horeb. It was his fear of God.

In his journey to Horeb, "The mount of God," Elijah was going back to where it all began. As Martin Buber suggests, he was returning "on Israel's tracks to the mountain of revelation"[10] to plead his case before Yahweh himself, the God of Israel. As he traveled "forty days and forty nights" (1 Kings 19:8) through the desert along the way, Elijah was following in the footsteps of Moses, Israel's very first spokesman and prophet. It was at Horeb that Israel was founded as a people and where the Lord had promised to be their God. It was at Horeb that the people of God entered into a covenant to "have no other gods" before him (Exodus 20:3). And it was at Horeb that the promise was broken in what would be the first of a seemingly endless list of betrayals.

Elijah was far from an accidental tourist when he arrived at Mt. Horeb; he was there on purpose. He had a grievance to file, and he was determined to appeal to the highest court in the land. When Elijah's words are read in their original context, the disappointment and disillusionment are palpable: "I have been very zealous for the LORD God Almighty. The Israelites have rejected your covenant, broken down your altars, and put your prophets to death with the sword. I am the only one left, and now they are trying to kill me too" (1 Kings 19:10).

This isn't what Elijah had signed up for. He had kept his part of the covenant, so why wasn't God keeping his? He had been faithful and obedient, and he had led the rest of God's people to renounce their infidelity and purge the land of their pagan oppressors. Was it unfair or unrealistic to expect God to keep his end of the bargain by subduing Israel's enemies under her feet, including the ruthless ringleader (Jezebel) herself? (See Exodus 20:20-33.) So what gives? If this was how things were going to be handled, Elijah would rather die than be party to it.

If there is an eerily familiar tone to these sentiments, it's because they have been spoken in some form by many other spiritual leaders through the ages. Having worked long and hard to lead the people of Israel out of bondage and into the Promised Land, Moses became increasingly disgusted by their perpetual resistance and by how he felt this reflected on his leadership. His complaint was similar to Elijah's: "If this is how you are going to treat me, please go ahead and kill me—if I have found favor in your eyes—and do not let me face my own ruin" (Numbers 11:15). When the Lord chose to extend mercy to Jonah's enemies instead of judgment, he expressed his disappointment with equal finality: "Now, LORD, take away my life, for it is better for me to die than to live" (Jonah 4:2-3). And then there is Job, of course, whose stoic expectations for personal vindication were repeatedly dashed by an escalating array of trials and temptations. Finally, when his disillusionment had reached its boiling point and he could take it no more, Job "opened his mouth and cursed the day of his birth"

(Job 3:1). This was a familiar refrain for Jeremiah as well, when his faithful proclamation of God's word was met with nothing but ridicule, insult, and reproach (Jeremiah 20:7-18). Each of these Bible heroes found themselves at a point of despair based on the fact that they were simply incapable of producing the results they had so earnestly anticipated. The path that descends from disappointment to disillusionment to despair is a slippery slope indeed.

## Defining Moments

Spiritual heroism inevitably breeds disillusionment because it is supremely results-oriented rather than relationship-oriented. Like modern comic book heroes, spiritual heroes are typically defined by their performance. A classic example of this can be found in a famous line from the 2005 film *Batman Begins*. When asked to reveal his true identity, the Dark Knight declares, "It's not who I am underneath, but what I do that defines me." The problem with this method of evaluating ourselves and others, including God, is not only that it fails to take into account the self-defeating perils of such a performance-based mentality, it also ignores the deeper realities that drive human behavior. While it is certainly true that we are all known by our fruit (Matthew 12:33), it is equally important to remember that the fruit of our lives is determined by the quality of our root system, for it is out of the overflow of the heart that the mouth speaks (Matthew 12:34). Since our heart is always rooted in relationship, it is the quality of our relationships that will ultimately determine the quality of our lives and ministries. "If you remain in me, . . . ." Jesus says, "you will bear much fruit; apart from me you can do nothing" (John 15:5). Belonging always precedes behaving.

This is one of the clearest and most liberating hallmarks of authentic Christianity: Followers of Jesus are not defined first and foremost by the level of their religious activity, but by the depth of their relational affiliation. Righteousness for the Christian is not based primarily on one's performance for God, but on one's personal encounter with God. Christianity must first be *received* before it can be *achieved*: "To all who did receive him, to those who believed in his name, he gave the right to become children of God" (John 1:12).

Literally speaking, to be a Christian is to be a "Christ one" or a "little Christ." Throughout the New Testament, members of the church are continually identified as those who are "in Christ" (Ephesians 1:1; Philippians 1:1; Colossians 1:2) because they are "loved by God" and "belong to Jesus Christ" (Romans 1:6-7). By the amazing grace of our Lord Jesus Christ, through the power of his Holy Spirit, we have been adopted into the family of God and have become co-heirs with Christ as sons and daughters of our heavenly Father (Romans 8:15-17). While it may sound too good to be true, this means that when the Father looks at each of us he declares the very same thing that he first announced to Jesus: "You are my [son or daughter], whom I love; with you I am well pleased" (Luke 3:22). This means that, through our relationship with Christ, we now have everything we could possibly need: Someone to belong to ("you are my son/daughter"), Someone to be loved by ("whom I love"), and Someone to believe in us ("with you I am well pleased"). The Christian life is not a product to be purchased; it is a revelation to be received.

With this in mind, it is fascinating to note that when God the Father affirmed Jesus as the glorious One through whom he would reveal his plan of redemption for the whole world, he would do so in a still, small voice on a mountaintop in the company of two divinely appointed companions, Moses and Elijah (Luke 9:28-36). This is the same Moses who asked to be "put to death" some fourteen hundred years earlier when faced with the overwhelming weight of leading God's people out of their bondage in Egypt. This is the same Elijah who "prayed that he might die" some eight hundred years earlier in light of his apparent failure to secure his people's release from the grip of Phoenician idolatry. And this is the same Moses and Elijah who experienced much-needed refreshment, renewal, and restoration in the presence of the living God.

Is it possible that as Moses and Elijah met with Jesus on the Mount of Transfiguration, and "spoke about his departure" (i.e., exodus), that they were there to reassure a weary Savior that his labor was not in vain? That in the face of constant opposition and sparse support, the Father had not abandoned him and would provide the strength to finish his task? Or was this theophany primarily intended to encourage Jesus' current traveling companions—Peter, James, and John—to keep the faith and stand firm in their allegiance to Jesus as Lord and Messiah, despite apparent evidence to the contrary? Could it be that these dozing disciples faced the same temptations that Moses and Elijah had faced during their years in spiritual leadership—including disillusionment and despair? And was this manifestation of God's glory in the presence of Christ intended to assure them that they were not crazy after all and to encourage them to see this journey to the end? And is it possible that the main point for Moses, Elijah, Jonah, Job, Jeremiah, Peter, James, John, and every other spiritual leader through the ages is that ultimately God is much more interested in our intimacy than in our productivity?[11]

As strange as it may seem, this painful experience of disillusionment would appear to be a prerequisite for the development of a genuinely intimate, sustainable faith. In fact, the very definition of disillusionment is "to be free of illusion or naïve faith and trust."[12] As one of my college professors was known to say, "Faith is fashioned in the workshop of doubt." Or as Peter Scazzero has put it, we must be willing to journey through the Wall:

> Emotionally healthy spirituality requires you to go through the pain of the Wall—or, as the ancients called it, "the dark night of the soul."
>
> This is God's way of rewiring and "purging our affections and passions" that we might delight in his love and enter into a richer, fuller communion with him. . . . He works to free us from unhealthy attachments and idolatries of the world. He longs for an intimate, passionate love relationship with us.

Going through the Wall breaks something deep within us—that driving, grasping, fearful self-will that must produce, that must make something happen, that must get it done for God (just in case he doesn't).[13]

## Rocky Mountain High

This truth became painfully and profoundly clear to me several years ago during my first attempt to "bag a fourteener"—to reach the summit of a fourteen-thousand-foot mountain peak. I was in my mid-forties at the time, and my knees were feeling the wear and tear that accompanies three or four decades of pounding up and down the basketball court. Indiana Jones once remarked during a memorable scene from *Raiders of the Lost Ark*, "It's not the years, it's the mileage." Actually, it's both.

I had done a fair bit of hiking and backpacking at that point in my life, but I really didn't know how well my body would hold up under the stress of such a strenuous climb. I figured if this was going to be my one shot at it I might as well go out in a blaze of glory, so I chose Mt. Elbert as my destination. At an elevation of 14,433 feet above sea level, Elbert is not only the highest point in Colorado (a state that is home to fifty-four of the country's sixty-six fourteeners), it is the tallest peak in the Rocky Mountains.

My climbing partner on this maiden voyage to the clouds was my eighteen-year-old son, Jeremiah. He was the only one of our six kids to be born in Colorado (the others were born in Ohio), so high country adventure was in his blood. We named him after the prophet Jeremiah, but we had Robert Redford's portrayal of *Jeremiah Johnson* in mind as well. Both monikers ring true.

When the moment of truth finally came, we could not have asked for more ideal climbing conditions. It was a picture-perfect day—clear, cool, and calm. With a belly full of buttermilk pancakes under our belts, we left the trailhead (elevation ten thousand feet) soon after sunrise. The first mile or two was relatively flat and shady. Above the timberline (approximately eleven thousand feet), the trail became a bit steeper, but our legs were still fairly fresh and the mountain air was exhilarating. After another mile or two, approaching twelve thousand feet, the path began to narrow, the air became noticeably thinner, and our breathing grew more labored. My knees began to make some noise at this point, both literally and figuratively. This required shorter steps, at least on my part, and more frequent water breaks. By the time we made it to thirteen thousand feet, the route suddenly morphed into a series of switchbacks, the pitch increased significantly, and the terrain became much more rugged. Movement was increasingly arduous. Forward progress slowed to a crawl. Our goal was now in view, but it seemed more daunting with each and every step.

Anyone who has climbed a fourteener will tell you that the last five hundred feet are often the most taxing. That was certainly the case with Elbert. My knees were barking loudly now, my lungs were burning, and my heart was pounding so hard I thought it would leap out of my chest. Exhaustion began to overtake me. My reserves were depleted, and my will was beginning to falter. I felt like I was on the verge of a total collapse. In the words of Peter Scazzero, I was "thrust up against the Wall."

Meanwhile, my teenage son was feeling the same effects but at a much lower level. He had been following my lead from the beginning, graciously slowing his pace in order to avoid passing me along the way. After quickly sizing up the situation, I made an executive decision. One of us had to make it to the top, and apparently, it wasn't going to be me. After much debate, I finally convinced Jeremiah to go on without me.

A short while later, my son arrived at the summit of Mt. Elbert, the crown jewel of the Colorado Rockies. He made it. He was on top of the world.

I will never forget what happened next. When I beheld my son standing on top of the mountain that day, so close and yet so far away, an unexpected surge of adrenaline suddenly washed over me, body and soul. Like someone who had just been jolted out of cardiac arrest with the assistance of a strategically applied electrical current, I was immediately revived, refreshed, and reinvigorated. Slowly but surely, I began to make my way up the remaining five hundred feet of trail until, much to my surprise, I found myself standing next to my son at the summit of Mt. Elbert. By the grace of God, I had bagged my first fourteener.

Jeremiah and I lingered longer than we anticipated that day, enjoying the spectacular view, taking photos, sharing a light lunch, and savoring a meaningful milestone together. As we eventually made our descent, I couldn't help but reflect upon this mountaintop experience, especially the supernatural power surge that enabled me to make it to the summit. What was that all about? And then it hit me: It wasn't primarily the thrill of victory, a sense of personal accomplishment, or a breathtaking panorama that inspired me to reach my destination that day. Simply stated, I couldn't bear the thought of being separated from my son. As drained and defeated as I may have felt, I was empowered to go through the Wall because I knew that Jeremiah was waiting for me on the other side. Personal achievement is not the ultimate motivator for human behavior. It's being with the one you love.

## A Gentle Whisper

Elijah hit the Wall at Mt. Horeb, and he hit it hard. He was "thrust up against it" as he made his way back on Israel's tracks to the mountain of revelation. Like so many others before and after him, Elijah grew disillusioned and got stuck along the way. And he surely would have dropped out altogether if not for one life-saving reality: God was waiting for him at the Wall.

Once again, the remedy that the Lord had to offer Elijah in the midst of his despair and disillusionment was probably not what he expected. What Elijah may have thought he needed was greater access to God's power. What the Lord knew Elijah needed was a greater awareness of his presence

(1 Kings 19:11a). More than anything, Elijah needed to be with God:

> Then a great and powerful wind tore the mountains apart and shattered the rocks before the LORD, but the LORD was not in the wind. After the wind there was an earthquake, but the LORD was not in the earthquake. After the earthquake came a fire, but the LORD was not in the fire. *And after the fire came a gentle whisper.* And when Elijah heard it, he pulled his cloak over his face and went out and stood at the mouth of the cave (1 Kings 19:11b-13a, emphasis mine).

The Hebrew phrase rendered here as "gentle whisper" has also been translated as a "still small voice" (KJV), a "soft gentle voice" (Darby), the "sound of a low whisper" (ESV), the "sound of a gentle blowing" (NASB), or even "a sound of sheer silence" (NRSV). Basically, modern translators are at a loss to conclusively describe this manifest presence of God. They shouldn't feel bad. So was Elijah. One of Israel's greatest spokesmen was at a complete loss for words. To borrow from Brennan Manning, he was "dazed, dumbstruck . . . and suddenly seized by the power of a great affection."[14] All he could do was stand in silent awe at the mouth of the cave, hanging on God's every word. It is amazing what God can do if preachers will just stop talking.

When we read the Gospels, it is interesting to note that a disciple is not called first to preach, teach, pray, heal, deliver, serve, lead, build, empower, or transform. According to Jesus, a disciple's first call is to "be with him" (see Mark 3:14; John 1:38-39). Good thing, too, because at the end of the day, this is also the only thing that cannot be taken away from us (see Luke 10:19-20, 41-42). Even our most powerful and persuasive ministries will one day cease, but his personal presence will never end: "I am with you always, to the very end of the age" (see Matthew 28:20; 1 Corinthians 13:8-13).[15]

There is no better remedy for disillusionment than dwelling in the presence of the Lord. When we hit the Wall, we can do nothing better than sit still and wait: "They that wait upon the Lord shall renew their strength; they shall mount up with wings as eagles; they shall run, and not be weary; and they shall walk, and not faint" (Isaiah 40:31 KJV). There is a God-shaped vacuum inside each one of us that cannot be filled by anything but God. Spiritual renewal is the only sure remedy for disillusionment.

## The Unforced Rhythms of Grace

This is why spiritual disciplines play such a critical role in the process of "waiting at the Wall."[16] While many of these renewing rituals have been central to the lives of Roman Catholic and Orthodox believers for centuries, there has been a welcome resurgence of interest in contemplative spirituality among evangelicals as well in recent years. Thanks in great part to the work of Richard Foster, the benefits of incorporating classic spiritual disciplines such as prayer, fasting, meditation, solitude, silence, confession, spiritual direction and Sabbath rest are becoming widely recognized once again as essential components in the ongoing practice of personal and spiritual renewal. As Foster stated, "The desperate need today is not for a greater number of intelligent people, or gifted people, but for deep people."[17]

Disillusionment does not discriminate. Every spiritual leader battles disillusionment at some point along the way. As in any marriage, there are predictable stages that we go through in our relationship with Christ. There is the honeymoon stage, the disillusionment stage, and the fulfillment stage. The key to overcoming the potentially fatal impact of disillusionment and experiencing a long and fulfilling life and ministry lies, in great part, in one's capacity for sustaining ongoing spiritual renewal. There is no substitute for the still, small voice of God.

As Jesus' own life and ministry demonstrates, this requires the intentional incorporation of a holy rhythm of engagement and withdrawal. It is illuminating to note that Jesus spent the first thirty years of his life in relative obscurity, quietly preparing for three short years of public ministry (see Luke 3:23). What's even more fascinating is that during these three years of intense engagement in service to others, the gospel writers tell us that Jesus made a regular habit of withdrawing to "lonely places" for prayer, often at the most unexpected and seemingly inopportune moments (see Luke 5:16). When he emerged from these periods of solitude, he typically returned to ministry with a renewed sense of passion and purpose, even more strenuously engaged in his messianic mission (see Luke 6:12-16; 9:10-17, 28-45; 11:1-28; 22:39–23:46). Unlike the crowds he sought to serve and the apostles he longed to lead, Jesus was called, not driven.[18]

Like Moses, Jesus knew the *shema* by heart: "*Hear*, O Israel: the LORD our God, the LORD is one" (Deuteronomy 6:4). Like Samuel, he had learned to pray, "Speak, LORD, for your servant is *listening*" (1 Samuel 3:9). Like David, he could testify, "My *ears* you have opened" (Psalm 40:6). And like Elijah, he knew how to recognize the "still small *voice* of God" (1 Kings 19:12 KJV).

Like Jesus, Christian leaders today must learn to listen well if we have any hope of discerning the call of God in this age of ever-increasing complexity and confusion. We must also learn to breathe. Just as the human respiratory system requires a balance of both inhalation and exhalation, so we must learn to practice the art of spiritual respiration. We must recognize our resistance to silence and solitude and renounce our propensity to work for God instead of with God.[19] This is the only reliable remedy for disillusionment, and the only sure cure for spiritual heroism. Like Jesus' first disciples, we too must learn "the unforced rhythms of grace" (Matthew 11:29 MSG).

# The Rhythms of Grace

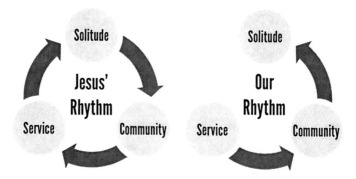

As this diagram[20] illustrates, we have too often reversed the rhythm that God revealed to us in and through Christ. Jesus' life and ministry were consistently rooted in his solitary communion with the Father, out of which he was prepared to enter into genuine community with his disciples, with whom he was fully equipped to serve the needs of the crowds (see Luke 6:12-17). In stark contrast, we tend to begin by passionately plunging into the great work of the gospel, which proves to be too much for any one of us on our own, forcing us to feverishly solicit the assistance of our fellow believers. This eventually wears them out as well, leaving everyone exhausted, disillusioned, and isolated as we each withdraw into our solitary fortresses of self-pity and self-protection. Is there any way out of this vicious cycle?

## Weekly Withdrawal

According to Eugene Peterson, translator of *The Message*, one of the best ways out of this mess is readily available for all those who are willing to enter in to the rest that is offered by God through the discipline of Sabbath-keeping:

> Every profession has sins to which it is especially liable. . . . I've had my eye on the snare from which pastors need deliverance: it is the sin of reversing the rhythms. Instead of grace/work we make it work/grace. Instead of working in a world in which God calls everything into being with his words and redeems his people with an outstretched arm, we rearrange it as a world in which we preach the mighty work of God and in afterthought ask him to bless our speaking.
>
> That, of course, is why so few pastors keep a Sabbath: we have reversed the rhythms. Perhaps that is why the Sabbath is *commanded*, not *suggested*, for nothing less than a command has the power to intervene in the vicious, accelerating, self-perpetuating cycle of faithless and graceless busyness, the only part of which we are conscious being our good intentions.
>
> Not many of us preach vigorously on the seventh commandment and then pursue lives of active adultery. But we conscientiously catechize our people on the fifth commandment and without a blush flaunt our workaholic Sabbath-breaking as evidence of an extraordinary piety.
>
> Sabbath-keeping: Quieting the internal noise so we hear the still, small voice of our

Lord. Removing the distractions of pride so we discern the presence of Christ.[21]

Not only is Sabbath-keeping one of the Ten Commandments (see Exodus 20:8-11)—universal standards given by God for the protection and provision of his people—but it is also one of the most effective ways to ward off the crippling effects of what Gordon MacDonald has called "The Sinkhole Syndrome":

> Sinkholes occur, scientists say, when underground streams drain away during seasons of drought, causing the ground at the surface to lose its underlying support. Suddenly everything caves in, leaving people with a frightening suspicion that nothing—not even the earth beneath their feet—is trustworthy.
>
> It is likely that at one time or another many of us have perceived ourselves to be on the verge of a sinkhole-like cave-in. In the feelings of numbing fatigue, a taste of apparent failure, or the bitter experience of disillusionment about goals or purposes, we may have sensed something within us about to give way. We feel we are just a moment away from a collapse that will threaten to sweep our entire world into a bottomless pit.[22]

Sadly, this is exactly what happened to MacDonald and his wife, Gail, in 1986, when it came to light that Gordon had entered into an extramarital affair with another woman, a scandal that sent shock waves throughout the evangelical community at the time. Far from discrediting his teaching on the importance of self-care and personal discipline, Gordon's moral failure only served to underscore the necessity of vigilance in these areas of spiritual leadership. Thankfully, the MacDonalds were able to survive this sinkhole in their personal lives and experience the restoration of their marriage and, to a great extent, their public ministry. Gordon continues to write and speak on the topic of personal and spiritual renewal, and he places Sabbath rest at the center of this discussion: "If my private world is in order, it will be because I have chosen to press Sabbath peace into the rush and routine of my daily life in order to find the rest God prescribed for Himself and all of humanity."[23] If God himself finds value in keeping the Sabbath, chances are it will be good for us as well (see Genesis 2:2-3; Exodus 20:8-11; Luke 4:16).

## Daily Devotion

Spiritual renewal also works its way into our lives as we take time to meditate on Scripture, the written word of God. As Jesus declared during his temptation in the wilderness, "Man shall not live on bread alone, but on every word that comes from the mouth of God" (Matthew 4:4). And it was his continual reliance on Scripture that empowered Christ to persevere throughout his public ministry, from beginning (Matthew 4:10) to end (Matthew 27:46). Spiritual leaders, like everything else in God's universe, are held together by the One who "*sustains* all things by his powerful word" (Hebrews 1:3 NRSV, emphasis mine).

This was certainly the case for G. Campbell Morgan, the Puritan preacher whose ministry spanned two continents and parts of two centuries (1863–1945). Inspired by D. L. Moody's first tour of England in 1873, Morgan preached his first sermon at the age of thirteen. But much like Elijah, he soon found himself engulfed in doubt and disillusionment concerning his faith and his call to ministry. Remembering those chaotic years, Morgan later wrote, "The only hope for me was the Bible. . . . I stopped reading books about the Bible and began to read the Bible itself. I saw the light and was back on the path."[24] For seven years thereafter he confined his reading concerning the things of God to the word of God itself. Once again, it was the still, small voice of God that spoke renewal and restoration into the life of this spiritual leader.

As the story goes, someone once asked G. Campbell Morgan, "Why is it that God does not speak to men today as he did to men of old?" Drawing, no doubt, from his countless hours of meditation on God's word, Morgan instinctively replied, "Perhaps the answer is that God has not stopped speaking at all, but that we have stopped listening to God as men of old once did."

One of the best ways to expand our capacity for hearing God's voice through Scripture is by practicing the ancient discipline of *lectio divina*, or sacred reading. In contrast to a modern, scientific approach to the study of Scripture in which we are encouraged to work on the text, this ancient practice emphasizes the importance of allowing the text to work on us. Like a cow chewing its cud, lectio divina provides a wonderful way to allow God's word to ruminate in our hearts and minds through a patient, contemplative reading of Scripture.

As spiritual leaders, we must be constantly reminded that there is a critical difference between the theological study of Scripture and the devotional reading of Scripture. It is entirely possible for pastors and other church leaders to devote endless hours to studying the word of God while failing to encounter the God of the word. The Bible is not simply a book of facts and figures; it is the story of God's relationship with his people. God's deepest desire is not merely to be understood, but to be adored and embraced.

## Continual Conversation

Prayer is another critical discipline for every spiritual leader who desires to hear and respond to the still, small voice of God. Nowhere is this more apparent than in the recent experience of the church in South Korea. It is no coincidence that the Korean church currently sends out more missionaries into the world than any country other than the United States (and they send far more per capita than we do!). Like every other great movement of God throughout the history of the Christian church, the current South Korean missionary movement is fueled by a passion for prayer. It is not uncommon for Korean pastors to spend four to five hours each day in prayer in order to be adequately prepared for the work that God has laid before them. This may also help to explain why ten of the eleven largest churches in the world are located in Seoul, the capital city of South Korea.[25]

Several years ago, I had the privilege of visiting Yoido Full Gospel Church in Seoul, reported to be the largest church in the world with a current membership of approximately one million people. More impressive than this staggering number, however, is the fact that nearly every one of these church members is being discipled through a vast and highly organized network of some one hundred thousand cell groups. When the founding pastor, David Yonggi Cho, was once asked to provide an explanation for the explosive growth and extraordinary impact that this church has experienced under his leadership over the past fifty years or so, he offered this simple yet profound reply: "I listen and I obey."

Throughout his life and ministry, Jesus demonstrated with unmistakable clarity that spiritual discernment is not so much an event as it is a continuing conversation. In what has often been referred to as "the praying gospel," Luke repeatedly testifies that it was "as he was praying" that Jesus heard the voice of God and made his power manifest among the people (see Luke 3:21; 6:12; 9:18, 29; 11:1; 22:32, 41; 23:34, 46). This reminds us that our capacity to hear God's voice in the midst of a spiritual crisis depends for the most part on how attentive we have been to his voice in our everyday routines. In other words, the clarity of each revelation from God will be directly dependent upon the quality of our relationship with God. "The conscious seeking of divine guidance," Dallas Willard argues, "is safe and sensible only within that life of experiential union with God in His Kingdom . . . only our communion with God provides the appropriate context of communications between us and Him."[26]

In his book, *Everything Belongs*, author Richard Rohr borrows the concept of kinesthetic knowing to describe the role of prayer in the shaping of our God-given calling and identity. "We know ourselves in the security of those who hold us and gaze upon us," Rohr summarizes, which he illustrates with the word picture of an infant gazing into his or her mother's eyes. "What her eyes tell us about ourselves, we believe and become. Prayer is much the same: we receive and return the divine gaze."[27]

As my good friend Fil Anderson is known to say, "There are as many ways to pray as there are moments in the day." So when it comes to the discipline of prayer, or to borrow from Richard Rohr's captivating illustration in the previous paragraph, prayer gazing, it would serve us well to remember that we are communicating with an omnipotent and supremely creative God who has unlimited resources at his disposal. This may help us to better understand and implement Paul's admonition to pray continually (1 Thessalonians 5:17). If the only tool we have in our prayer toolbox is intercession, for example, this would appear to be an impossible command to fulfill. But when we realize that our Lord has supplied us with a seemingly endless assortment of additional prayer tools—contemplative prayer, fixed hours of prayer, the Lord's prayer, prayers of examen, prayer songs, prayer walks, flash prayers, breath prayers, concerts of prayer, just to name a few—we soon discover that the call to "pray continually" is much more than a dutiful obligation. It is a divine invitation to continually practice the presence of God as we learn to pray always by praying in all ways. It also frees us from the stranglehold of legalism as we experience increasing freedom to pray as we can, not as we can't.[28]

As indicated earlier, there is a plethora of additional disciplines at our disposal as well, and it is likely that each of us will benefit from incorporating any number of them into a uniquely crafted rule of life.[29] But at the end of the day, Christian tradition, based on the example of Jesus himself, clearly demonstrates that there is no substitute for the essential and life-giving disciplines of Sabbath-keeping (weekly withdrawal), Scripture reading (daily devotion), and prayer gazing (continual conversation), in all of their varied expressions. Taken together, they provide each of us with a solid, reliable, three-legged stool upon which we can rest our weary souls as we wait upon the Lord to renew our strength and restore to us the joy of our salvation.

## An Audience of One

The ultimate purpose behind each of these disciplines and many others is to help us hear and respond to the still, small voice of God. This, in turn, enables us to ignore other competing voices, both internal and external, so that we might be empowered to overcome despair and disillusionment as we live and serve before an "Audience of One":

A life lived listening to the decisive call of God

is a life lived before the audience that trumps all others—the Audience of One. . . . [Like the Puritans before us] we who live before the Audience of One can say to the world: "I have only one audience. Before you I have nothing to prove, nothing to gain, nothing to lose."

Needless to say, the modern world is light years from the Puritan world. We have moved from the "inner directed" world of the Puritans, in which calling acted as an inner compass, to the "other directed" world of modern society, in which our contemporaries are our real guides—and a roving radar ranges to pick up their cues. . . . The Puritans lived as if they had swallowed gyroscopes; we modern Christians live as if we have swallowed Gallup polls.[30]

It might be helpful to close this discussion on the importance of listening with a parable. There is a legend from the Old West about a group of prospective telegraph operators who were seeking employment with the Union Pacific Railroad. When the day to be interviewed for this prestigious position finally arrived, each of these men gathered in a large waiting room outside of the director's office, eagerly anticipating the opportunity to showcase their respective qualifications for the job. After waiting together for a short time, one of the youngest applicants suddenly stood up from the back of the room and walked right into the director's office. A few minutes later, this same young man returned to the waiting room, with the director following close behind. "I have an announcement to make," the director declared. "We have found the right man for the job. Thank you all for your interest. You are free to go."

Shocked and dismayed by this sudden turn of events, the remaining applicants felt like they had been routinely dismissed without receiving a fair hearing. One of the more experienced applicants promptly rose to his feet to register his complaint with the director: "I beg your pardon, sir, but this situation is completely unacceptable. Many of us have been working for years just to be considered for this job, and yet when one of the youngest and least experienced among us strolls uninvited into your office you casually dismiss our collective resources and give the job to this amateur instead. With all due respect, I believe we deserve an explanation!"

"Certainly," the director replied, "the explanation is actually quite simple. While you were all sitting in the waiting room, I was sitting in my office sending the following message over the telegraph: 'If you can hear this message, come into my office immediately. The job is yours.' This young man's response clearly demonstrated his unique qualifications for the job."

The "still, small voice of God" is not limited to momentary, mountain-top experiences. God is always speaking. The only question is—are we listening?

## Making it Personal

1. Where do you see evidence of the "I'm too busy" syndrome in your life?

2. What prevents you from keeping the schedule you would like to keep?

3. What feelings are stirred as you think about time and Sabbath rest?

4. By God's grace, what practical steps can you take today to start or strengthen the holy habits that will help you to live more freely and fully before an audience of one?

# Chapter Three
## The Rhythm of Vocational Realignment:
## A Remedy for Isolation

*Go back the way you came . . . and anoint Elisha son of
Shaphat.* (1 Kings 19:15-16)

## The Game Changer

The final score was embarrassing. The stat line was
pitiful. It was yet another lopsided defeat at the hands
of a beatable foe. It felt like the 1979-80 high school
basketball season would never end, and we were only
halfway through the schedule.

No loss is easy to swallow, but I was taking this
one particularly hard. I felt personally responsible.
I was supposed to be the game changer, after all. I
was the big city kid who had transferred to this little
town on the prairie, supposedly bringing with me a
peach basket full of street smarts, smooth moves,
and other enviable skills that would magically trans-
port my adopted team to a new level of athletic
glory. At least that was what I told myself.

Now I was sitting in the passenger seat of my
dad's '79 Olds Cutlass, riding home from the game

in complete silence. It was going to be a very long drive.

After several miles of uneasy silence, my dad's voice finally broke the stalemate.

"Do you want to quit?"

It sounded like a purely rhetorical question at that point. Of course I wanted to quit. A couple of other players had already done so, and it was hard to find a good reason not to join them. But there was no way I was going to attempt to offer a verbal response to the question. I was so upset that I knew if I tried to talk I would probably just burst into tears, adding even more insult to injury.

Again, it was my dad's voice that gently waded into the void.

"Well, David, I just want you to know that whether you quit or not, your mom and I will love you the same."

More powerful and life-giving words have never been spoken. In a moment pregnant with potential, for better or for worse, I was the beneficiary of pure, undiluted grace. It was being poured all over me like the sweetest honey from heaven.

In the blink of an eye, it seemed, I was jolted out of my suffocating self-pity. I was loved. I always had been, and I always would be. And this was based not in my fleeting performance, but in an enduring relationship with one who knew me, warts and all, and loved me anyway. I had nothing to prove and nothing to lose.

Make no mistake. It was my dad's voice speaking to me that day. But somehow, mysteriously, I knew in my heart at that moment that the words ultimately came from somewhere, and from someone much greater. Like Elijah and Brennan Manning before me, I, too found myself "dazed, dumbstruck . . . and suddenly seized by the power of a great affection."[1]

I don't remember anything about the conversation after that. As far as I know, neither one of us spoke another word on the drive home that night. All I can tell you is this: my father's unconditional love empowered me to persevere. I not only finished out the season, but according to those who knew me at the time, I was enabled to do so with an unusual level of Christ-like grace, peace, and poise. Much to my surprise, some twenty years later I received an email from one of my former teammates telling me that he had decided to follow Jesus based primarily upon the work of Christ he witnessed in me during our time together on and off the court that year as high school seniors.

Talk about a game changer.

## Calling and Community

If it is true that we have been called to live and serve before an audience of one, it is also true that we have been created to do so among a wider community of companions. There are times when every spiritual leader needs a cave, and there are times when every spiritual leader needs a tribe as well.

Like Frodo Baggins, the unlikely hero in Tolkien's *Lord of the Rings* trilogy, every disciple of Jesus has been given a great mission to accomplish. And like Frodo, we quickly discover that we are going to need a lot of help along the way. Thankfully, God does not expect us to follow him on our own, and he graciously provides us with a fellowship of faithful traveling companions to encourage us and remind us of our mission when we are tempted to give up hope, just as my dad did for me on that memorable drive home so many years ago. As Dietrich Bonhoeffer learned firsthand during his years in an underground seminary in Nazi Germany, "The Christian needs another Christian who speaks God's Word to him. . . . He needs his brother solely because . . . the Christ in his own heart is weaker than the Christ in the word of his brother; his own heart is uncertain, his brother's is sure."[2]

No one would have known this better than Elijah. While his battle with spiritual heroism was certainly assuaged through the Lord's gracious provision of physical refreshment and spiritual renewal, the struggle was far from over. Ironically, just as Jezebel raised her voice in protest following Israel's apparent victory at Mt. Carmel, so Elijah raised his own voice in protest in the midst of his personal victory at Mt. Horeb. There was a remnant of resistance in the air, even in the face of Yahweh's dramatic self-revelation to the disillusioned prophet, and Elijah felt compelled to repeat his previous complaint:

> Then a voice said to him, "What are you doing here, Elijah?" He replied, "I have been

very zealous for the LORD God Almighty. The Israelites have rejected your covenant, torn down your altars, and put your prophets to death with the sword. *I am the only one left,* and now they are trying to kill me too" (1 Kings 19:13b-14, emphasis mine).

Like so many other spiritual leaders before and after him, Elijah experienced the final, and perhaps the most perilous phase in the process of burnout: isolation. The devastating effects of exhaustion and disillusionment had taken their toll, and he was reeling from their impact. Like a prize fighter after a fifteen-round brawl with a heavyweight contender, Elijah was still recovering in his corner of the ring. Bruised and battered from the fight, consumed by the weight of his own wounds, Elijah seemed unable or unwilling to receive the full benefits of Yahweh's restoration and renewal. It would seem that his focus had become so fixated on his own weariness and pain that he was blinded to the greater realities around him. Elijah's victory over the plague of spiritual heroism would not be complete until he received one last gift from the Lord, the gift of vocational realignment:

The Lord said to him, "Go back the way you came, and go to the Desert of Damascus. When you get there, anoint Hazael king over Aram. Also, anoint Jehu son of Nimshi king over Israel, and anoint Elisha son of Shaphat from Abel Meholah to succeed you as prophet. Jehu will put to death any who escape the sword of Hazael, and Elisha will put to death any who escape the sword of Jehu. *Yet I reserve seven thousand in Israel*—all whose knees have not bowed down to Baal and all whose mouths have not kissed him."

So Elijah went from there and found Elisha. . . . Elijah went up to him and threw his cloak around him. Elisha then left his oxen and ran after Elijah. . . . He set out to follow Elijah and became his servant (1 Kings 19:15-21, emphasis mine).

Pity parties are never pretty, and they are never fun. They tend to be extremely lonely affairs. Like Elijah, however, even the best of us can become easily entangled in the what's-in-it-for-me trap. While this has been a temptation for every generation of spiritual leaders, it could easily be argued that we currently live in one of the most self-absorbed eras in human history. As Len Sweet once quipped, "We can't even spell Wii® without using two I's." Narcissism is one of the unavoidable side-effects of spiritual heroism:

We tend to become so concerned with doing something worthwhile, bringing about changes . . . that we often seem to forget that it is not we who redeem, but God. . . . We then have forgotten that our vocation is not to give visibility to our powers but to God's . . . when our own needs begin to dominate our actions, long-range service becomes difficult and we soon become exhausted, burned out, and even embittered by our efforts.[3]

Our human need for recognition and acceptance, if not met in and through Christ alone, can easily lead us to a place where we are apt to use our service to others as an attempt to satisfy these un-met needs in our own lives. Most of us have been there and done that, and we have discovered the hard way that it always leaves us "exhausted, burned out, and . . . embittered." By God's grace, he allows us to see this for what it is, and his kindness leads us to a place of repentance and restoration.

A central part of this restoration process hinges on our willingness to recognize our deep, God-given need to share our lives and ministries with others. Our identity as men and women of God and as ministers of the gospel is forged in the fires of friendship. It is through the rubric of relationship that we sift through the complex array of internal and external voices that bombard us every day, each one attempting to reshape our self-worth and re-define our destiny. And it is in the context of com-munity that we seek to discern the still, small voice of God calling us to embrace or resume our respec-tive vocations. This helps to explain why isolation can become such a destructive force in the lives of spiritual leaders:

> We are able to do many hard things, tolerate many conflicts, overcome many obstacles, and persevere under many pressures, but when we no longer experience ourselves as part of a caring community, we quickly lose faith. This is because faith in God's compassionate pres-ence can never be separated from experienc-ing God's presence in the community to which we belong . . . apart from a vital relationship with a caring community a vital relationship with Christ is not possible.[4]

Unfortunately, we know very little about Elijah's community of origin. The biblical record just does not give us much to work with. He suddenly appears on the scene with this terse introduction: "Elijah the Tishbite, from Tishbe in Gilead" (1 Kings 17:1). Who were his parents? Was he an orphan? Was he married? Did he have children? What did he do for a living? Was he respected by his friends and neighbors? Some scholars have speculated that his origins in Gilead may indicate that he was not an Israelite but an Ishmaelite, citing the appointment of a gentile to such an extraordinary place of leadership as an open rebuke intended to shame the apostate people of Israel.[5] But this is pure conjecture. All we know for sure is that "Elijah was a human being just like us" (James 5:17 NCV), i.e., he was an ordinary person from an ordinary place who lived at an ordinary time in human history. And just like the rest of us, he was endowed by his Creator with an innate need for community (see Genesis 2:18).

The fact that we have so little information on Elijah's background may actually help us understand why he was prone to the perils of isolation. It seems apparent that he was somewhat of a loner and wanderer by nature. While he was not unique among the prophets in this regard, these qualities seem to be accentuated more than most in Elijah's life and ministry. Even Jeremiah, "the weeping prophet," had the advantages of priestly parenting (Hilkiah, Jeremiah 1:1), reliable assistance (Baruch, Jeremiah 32:12; 36:4-32), and royal support (Josiah, Jeremiah 1:2). The only ally that is mentioned by name in Elijah's case is Obadiah, a "devout believer in the Lord" who rescued at least one hundred of Yahweh's prophets from certain death while serving as an overseer in Ahab's palace (1 Kings 18:3-4). This fact in itself underscores the myopic perspective that dominated Elijah's mindset at Mt. Horeb, where the lonely prophet erroneously lamented that he was "the only one left" (1 Kings 19:10, 14).

## Being Known

Americans are among the loneliest people in the world.[6] What's more, according to the results of a study published in the *American Sociological Review*, Americans have become even lonelier and more isolated in recent years. In 1985, the average American had three people in whom they could confide matters important to them. By 2004, that number had dropped to two, and 25 percent of those surveyed had no close confidants at all.[7]

If this growing experience of loneliness and isolation presents serious challenges for the body of Christ as a whole, then it is fair to say that these challenges are only accentuated for those serving in places of spiritual leadership, many of whom are struggling with burnout due primarily to a lack of interpersonal intimacy. This is confirmed by the data presented earlier indicating that 70 percent of pastors do not have anyone in their lives whom they would consider a close friend. As well-educated, Bible college and seminary-trained church leaders, we have been thoroughly catechized in the business of knowing, but we are woefully and dangerously ignorant when it comes to the art of being known:

> Our Western world has long emphasized knowledge—factual information and "proof"—over the process of being known by God and others. No wonder then, that despite all our technological advances and the proliferation of social media, we are more intra- and interpersonally isolated than ever. Yet it is only when we are known that we are positioned to become conduits of love. And it is love that transforms our minds, makes forgiveness possible, and weaves a community of disparate people into the tapestry of God's family.[8]

Based on their work with hundreds of clergy over the years, Donald Hands and Wayne Fehr have concluded that "the experience of intimacy is the core of health and salvation" for every spiritual leader.[9] Both men are ordained Episcopal priests themselves, and together they have provided over ten thousand hours of spiritual direction and psychotherapy to men and women from a wide variety of denominational backgrounds. In their writings on clergy health, Hands and Fehr continually emphasize the "indispensable function of community in enabling and sustaining the individual's movement of recovery," a process through which "a person who has been emotionally isolated gradually learns to become interdependent with others" instead of "attempting to be god of his or her own universe."[10]

Psychologists William Grosch and David Olsen have invested a great deal of time and energy in the study of clergy burnout as well. Like Hands and Fehr, they would affirm the need for greater interpersonal intimacy among spiritual leaders. They would also add that this nagging sense of disconnectedness begs for a deeper understanding of family systems:

> The work environment, and particularly the church, can become a type of second family, resulting in even seasoned professionals responding to their work environment in the same ways as they related to their family of origin. . . . As anxiety increases, old family-of-origin patterns return. . . . As clergy better understand their needs for validation and praise, as well as understand the way they have internalized old family maps, they then are in a better position to define themselves differently, and in so doing deal with these forces differently. They then are far less likely to burnout.[11]

Throughout my thirty years of personal experience in pastoral ministry, I have discovered firsthand that finding and building supportive family systems with other church leaders in a local community can be a very difficult and daunting process as well. The sad but true reality is that most pastors do not trust each other. Not only do we too often see ourselves in competition with each other, but we are rarely willing or able to invest the time necessary to build close, personal friendships with peers in our area. On one level, this may serve as yet another call to repentance, but it also speaks to the critical need for spiritual leaders to invest themselves intentionally, and often sacrificially, in the cultivation of intimate friendships with at least a handful of safe companions:

> Most clergy are relatively isolated, emotionally and spiritually, without enough *peer* support. They stand alone, as helpers to others, but are not appreciated or affirmed as equals. . . . Participating in a genuine spiritual community as an equal is very important for a cleric's health and well-being. . . . Clergy who recognize that they are relatively isolated need to take the initiative to find or create the kind of peer spiritual community in which they can live and grow.

Although such peer friendship may sound wonderful in theory, it is much harder to find this type of trusting, transparent community in the real world of market-driven ministry in which today's spiritual leaders live and move and have their being. As a general rule, most pastors and other church leaders have had very little experience with genuine intimacy in any context, including their relationships with God, themselves, and with their own families.[12]

In 2005, a team of clinical psychologists at George Fox University, under the leadership of Mark McMinn, conducted a comprehensive review of several recent studies that examined ways pastors and their spouses attempt to cope with the exceptional stress that accompanies local church ministry. Their findings revealed some clear patterns:

> Community resources appear sparse for many clergy. Though clergy desire and need friendships, many have difficulty forming close relationships outside their immediate family

because they perceive themselves to be "put on a pedestal" (viewed as paragons of Christian virtue) and "boxed in" by parishioners' expectations of ways pastors should behave. These expectations can have an isolating effect. For example, a pastor having a difficult day may be expected to pray about it, whereas a surgeon may have a drink or two with his coworkers. Moreover, parishioners may disapprove of pastors who form exclusionary or special relationships with congregation members. As a result, clergy sometimes experience relationships that lack depth and intimacy.

In their conclusion, the authors noted that most pastors have access to a variety of intrapersonal coping resources (prayer, Bible reading, exercise, hobbies), and many are able to draw strength from their marriage and family relationships, but few of these spiritual leaders mentioned interactions outside of their families (friendships, mentoring, accountability) as a primary coping resource. Although these conclusions may be sobering, a hopeful note was struck as well in the authors' assertion that "coaching with pastors is a promising area of clergy-psychologist collaboration" in that it "allows pastors to establish an important collegial relationship with a helping colleague." It also has practical advantages over supervisory relationships with denominational officials because "coaches are not in evaluative and decision-making roles with authority over pastors."[13]

Sheri Ferguson is a licensed social worker who serves as the executive director of North Alabama Methodist Pastoral Care and Counseling. Based on her extensive study and experience, Ferguson offers the following summary: "Research has determined that pastors who cultivate relationships with friends, family, colleagues, support systems/mentors, and consultants have lower incidences of depression and burnout."[14]

## A Call for Soft Individualism

In his book, *The Different Drum: Community Making and Peace*, best-selling author and Harvard-trained psychiatrist Scott Peck summarizes the challenges and opportunities before us as we seek ways to reconstruct meaningful relationships in the midst of a splintering society:

> Trapped in our tradition of rugged individualism, we are an extraordinarily lonely people . . . We are desperately in need of a new ethic of "soft individualism," an understanding of individualism which teaches that we cannot be truly ourselves until we are able to share freely the things we most have in common: our weakness, our incompleteness, our imperfection, our inadequacy, our sins, our lack of wholeness and self-sufficiency. . . . It is the kind of softness that allows those necessary barriers, or outlines, of our individual selves to be like permeable membranes, permitting ourselves to seep out and the selves of others to seep in. It is the kind of individualism that acknowledges our interdependence not merely in the intellectual catchwords of the day but in the very depths of our hearts. It is the kind of individualism that makes real community possible.[15]

For Peck, the concept of "soft individualism" is rooted in a formative experience that took place some thirty-five years before he was able to articulate these words. In the fall of 1952, Peck began his junior year in high school at Friends Seminary, a Quaker prep school on the edge of Greenwich Village in New York City. Despite tremendous diversity within the student body, Peck has no memory of any cliques, outcasts, divisiveness or any unusual pressure to be anything other than himself. What was most memorable about his two years at Friends Seminary, Peck recounts, is that "all the boundaries between people were soft."[16]

Rick Warren, pastor of Saddleback Church and author of the hugely popular *Purpose-Driven Life*, is well known for rattling off memorable aphorisms. This is one of his best: "Our strengths breed competition, but our weaknesses build community." What a profound statement and what a prophetic word to those who serve as leaders in the body of Christ today. As studies have repeatedly indicated, the greatest barrier to community building among pastors is the fear of judgment. This paralyzing fear is regularly reinforced through competition with our peers, criticism from our supervisors, and conflict with our congregations. But when we are willing to confront this fear, stepping forward with courage to confess our weakness, our brokenness, and our neediness before our brothers and sisters in Christ, the power of soft individualism is immediately unleashed:

> In confession the break-through to community takes place. Sin demands to have a man by

himself. It withdraws him from the community. The more isolated a person is, the more destructive will be the power of sin over him, and the more deeply he becomes involved in it, the more disastrous his isolation.

In confession the light of the Gospel breaks into the darkness and seclusion of the heart. . . . The expressed, acknowledged sin has lost all its power. . . . It can no longer tear the fellowship asunder. . . . The sin concealed separated him from the fellowship, made all his apparent fellowship a sham; the sin confessed has helped him to find true fellowship with the brethren of Jesus Christ.[17]

Dietrich Bonhoeffer's pastoral concerns regarding the destructive and potentially disastrous impact of isolation are well-founded, according to psychiatrist Gerald May. As director of spiritual guidance at the Shalem Institute in Washington DC, May served as a counselor, companion, and caring friend for multitudes of spiritual leaders until his death in 2005. An expert on the dynamics of addiction, May has observed that addictive behaviors always thrive best in hiding (see Genesis 3:8, 10). Even when "addicts are no longer able to avoid the truth about their own behavior," May states, "it becomes increasingly important to hide it from other people. Now the addictive behavior becomes more secretive." This, in turn, leads to "an increasing sense of self-alienation, and a growing isolation from other people. There is a sense of harboring a dark secret, the revelation of which would be unbearable."[18] This may help to explain why secret sin is so rampant within Christian community.

Similar sentiments are expressed by psychologist Archibald Hart. Having worked extensively with members of the clergy throughout his career, Hart identifies depression as a primary vocational hazard for spiritual leaders. "The pastor's life is marked by a type of loneliness that is peculiar to those who receive their calling from God," Hart concedes, but this "solitude of sacredness" can quickly degenerate into a "defensive, self-protecting false independence" that can leave these leaders cut off from necessary support systems. Hart warns that "if steps are not deliberately taken to develop these trusting and supportive relationships in each pastorate, the loneliness of leadership responsibilities will lead to isolation and a distortion of reasoning—and this spells depression for many ministers."[19]

## Two Are Better Than One

Clearly the road to recovery cannot be traveled alone. We must take public transportation, so to speak. As Cyprian, bishop of Carthage, has testified, "He cannot have God for his father who has not the Church for his mother."

"Two are better than one," a wise man once said, "if either of them falls down, one can help the other up. . . . Though one may be overpowered, two can defend themselves. A cord of three strands is not quickly broken" (Ecclesiastes 4:9-10, 12). Does this mean that two friends constitute a complete community? In a very real and biblical sense, the answer may be yes. Jesus promised, "Where two or three gather in my name, there am I with them" (Matthew 18:20). Based on the teaching of both the Old and New Testaments, then, we can say way with confidence that there is always a minimum of two or three in every authentic expression of Christian community.

This is a beautiful reflection of our triune God himself, in whose image we have each been created: "Let *us* make human beings in *our* image" (Genesis 1:27 MSG, emphasis mine). According to Genesis, to be created "in the image and likeness of God" is to be formed for community, based on the reality that God essentially functions as a holy community—Father, Son, Spirit.[20] Community is inseparable from godliness because community is inherent in the very nature of God.

In *The Search to Belong*, Joseph Myers draws heavily from the work of American anthropologist Edward T. Hall in his appeal to rethink the way that we understand and practice community. In the 1960s, Hall developed a theory based on the relationship between space and culture. He coined the term *proxemics* "for the interrelated observations and theories of man's use of space." He concluded that there are four spaces we use to develop personalities, culture, and communication: public, social, personal, and intimate. "Belonging is multi-dimensional," Myers concludes, because "people belong to us on different levels."[21]

So how can a spiritual leader take intentional steps to avoid the pitfalls of isolation and cultivate genuine community with fellow traveling companions? Much like a car that has been jarred out of alignment over time due to misuse, neglect, or head-on collision, our relationships are frequently jarred out of alignment as well. A basic strategy for vocational realignment, then, will require us to re-examine, reinforce and/or repair relationships in each of the four spaces in our lives.

First, we must pay closer attention to those with whom we share public space. Jesus loves the whole world (John 3:16), and so must we. Granted, this becomes an ever more weighty challenge in an age of information overload. It is increasingly tempting to draw away from the global community in an effort to conserve our limited time and energy. But we do so at great peril to our own souls. Self-care can easily disintegrate into self-protection. Left unchecked, self-protection can quickly morph into full-blown narcissism. We must fight the temptation to withdraw from the world completely and become cloistered away in seemingly safe, secure, self-made cocoons. We must remain meaningfully engaged with our neighbors, both near and far. If not, we run the risk of ending up like Elijah, curled up in a ball, whining that he was the only one left. People wrapped up in themselves make very small and pitiful packages indeed.

Second, we must build mutually supportive social networks among our peers. Jesus was fully divine, yes, but he was also fully human. If he needed a team of at least seventy others to share the load with him, then it is likely that each of us will need at least that many in our own lives. By consulting regularly with ministry partners and supervisors we benefit from their wisdom, encouragement, and admonition. It is helpful to keep a referral list and use it wisely. We must learn to delegate responsibility and develop leadership teams through shared ministry, and continue to build new relationships through participation in ministerial associations, conferences, retreats, and continuing education opportunities.

Third, we must cultivate authentic fellowship with those whom we consider close, personal friends. The folks who wrote the theme song for *Cheers* were right: "Sometimes you want to go where everybody knows your name." Jesus had the Twelve, of course, a small band of brothers (complemented by a number of dear sisters) who ate, slept, traveled, served, laughed, and lived together day in and day out. In the same way, each of us must seek to develop close, personal relationships with family and friends, people we know and trust, in order to give and receive mutual encouragement, support, and accountability (or better yet, "edit-ability"[22]). As Hands and Fehr suggest, we must make sure to maintain non-professional friendships, "out of role and responsibility," with people who love and accept us just as we are, based on our relationship with them, not our performance for them. I have become personally convinced that every spiritual leader would benefit from meeting regularly with a mentor, counselor, or spiritual director as well. We all need a trusted confidant, soul friend, or sacred companion to walk alongside us on our journey.

Fourth, we must invest heavily and intentionally in our most intimate relationships. Jesus modeled this in his relationship with Peter, James, and John. As Charles Stanley once said, "I found God doesn't have favorites, but He does have intimates." There are just some people in our lives with whom we have a special chemistry or affinity. These soul mates are special gifts from God. If we are married, this inner circle will certainly include our spouses, but there is no reason to limit spiritual intimacy to the bonds of matrimony. Elijah had Elisha. Moses had Joshua, David had Jonathan, Naomi had Ruth, Paul had Timothy. On the deepest level, it is in the context of this intimate space where we are invited to enter into what the New Testament writers refer to as genuine *koinonia*, a participation or sharing together in the very life of Christ himself.

As noted earlier, this is the most vital yet difficult, and therefore most neglected space in the lives of most spiritual leaders. Let's face it. Intimacy is a risky business. It requires vulnerability and transparency, two of the scariest words in a leader's personal vocabulary. Many of us would rather die than share our deepest hopes, fears, sorrows, and secrets with another human being. But it should be clear by now that the risks associated with a lack of intimacy are great. The reality is that those who refuse to share their lives openly with anyone at any time under any circumstances are already in trouble.

## Reverse Mentoring

One could argue that Elijah's life was saved by the re-
demptive power of community. It certainly extended
his ministry career. Crushed by the overwhelming
weight of exhaustion, disillusionment, and isolation,
Elijah ran away from home, as far and as fast as his
weary legs could carry him, rushing headlong into
the desert with a death wish in hand. What he found
must have surprised him. Like so many others before
and after him—Moses, David, John the Baptist, Jesus,
Paul, Antony—it was in the desolation of the desert
that Elijah found the essence of life. And it was in
the most solitary of surroundings that he found true
fellowship.

Touched by a compassionate angel of the Lord,
Elijah received the gift of physical refreshment as a
remedy for his exhaustion (1 Kings 19:5-8). Moved
by the gentle presence of the Lord, Elijah received
the gift of spiritual renewal as a remedy for his
disillusionment (1 Kings 19:9-14). Attended by a
humble servant of the Lord, Elijah received the gift
of vocational realignment as a remedy for his isolation (1 Kings 19:15-21). He was not the only one
left after all.

Apparently, this divinely appointed bond between Elijah and Elisha served them quite well
throughout their years of partnership in ministry.
While we do not have lengthy descriptions of the
exact nature of their relationship, it is clear from the
biblical record that they developed a deep love and
admiration for one another. From their first encounter, it is evident that Elijah was fully vested in this

relationship. Throwing his cloak around his newly appointed apprentice, the prophetic mantle was officially passed to a new generation of leadership. Although Elijah's ministry was far from over, it may have been a bittersweet moment for the battle-worn Tishbite, a moment pregnant with both relief and regret. At his young successor's request, Elijah encouraged Elisha to offer a final farewell to his parents before he left the family farm for good. With newfound tenderness and compassion in his voice, the seasoned ministry veteran consented, "Go back. . . . For what have I done to you?" (1 Kings 19:20). While translators offer varying opinions as to the exact meaning of this expression, it would not be difficult to imagine Elijah, based on his own experience in ministry, granting Elisha's request with a slight turn of the head as he whispers under his breath, "What have I gotten you into!"

As is often the case, Elijah surely received as much or more than he invested in this prophetic partnership. After all, it required no small sacrifice for Elisha to accept the invitation to serve a new master. Anyone living in his day who was wealthy enough to own twelve yoke of oxen had much to lose, at least from an earthly perspective. Yet Elisha eagerly embraced his new vocation, having counted the cost, and like Jesus' first disciples, left everything behind to follow the Lord's call to ministry in the company of his esteemed mentor. Elisha humbly devoted himself to Elijah as his personal servant, the one who would "pour water on the hands" of his mentor (1 Kings 19:21; 2 Kings 3:11).

But by far the most poignant expression of Elisha's affection for Elijah is found in the final chapter of their partnership. As Elisha's beloved master prepares for his departure from this world, a reality that his prophetic companions see fit to constantly remind the young apprentice, Elisha repeatedly reaffirms his vow of unwavering devotion: "As surely as the Lord lives and as you live, I will not leave you" (2 Kings 2:2, 4, 6). As they are about to be separated from each other, Elisha makes one last request, asking Elijah to allow him to "inherit a double portion of your spirit" (to receive the blessing of the firstborn, in this case, to be a full heir or successor of the prophetic office and gifts of his master)[23]—yet another indication of his utmost respect and admiration for Elijah. Finally, as his friend and mentor is taken up to heaven in a whirlwind, Elisha's truest sentiments are revealed: "My father! My father! The chariots and horsemen of Israel!" And then he was gone (2 Kings 2:12).

Grief must have been overwhelming for Elisha that day. But in the days that followed, it became clear to everyone that the apprentice had indeed received a double portion of his master's spirit (2 Kings 2:15). Elisha had received infinitely greater blessing through his relationship with Elijah than any amount of earthly wealth could possibly provide. And what did Elijah receive from Elisha? Hope. Help. Healing. And an enduring legacy that he couldn't have imagined, even in his wildest dreams. A legacy that was no longer bound by the baggage of spiritual heroism. By the grace of God, Elijah received the gift of reverse mentoring:

> Tapping the wisdom of the young requires that missional leaders go off road to develop reverse mentoring relationships, a very specific form of friendship in which the junior instructs the senior, not as a replacement for other forms of mentoring but as an essential complement to them.

> Reverse mentoring opens up the possibility of a relationship in which both participants simultaneously teach and learn, each making the other an adopted peer. "As iron sharpens iron, so one man sharpens another." Strictly one-way mentoring (upward or downward) resembles iron sharpening wood: all the power is on the side of the person whittling the other into his image. But with iron on both sides, each can be sharpened or conformed into the image of Christ through the work of the Spirit in the relationship.[24]

## Passing the Baton

When we consider the significance of the ministry entrusted to those of us called to serve as spiritual leaders in the body of Christ, we can give thanks for the "great cloud of witnesses" (Hebrews 12:1) who modeled the Christian life before us. This includes well-known saints through the ages, of course, but it also includes those lesser-known parents, spouses, pastors, professors, mentors, coaches, colleagues, and friends who have been influential in the shaping of our lives and ministries. We can be encouraged to remember that we, like Elijah and many others before us, have been given the great privilege and awesome responsibility of passing the baton:

> The off-road discipline of baton passing . . . will be required if we are to develop a cooperative relationship between the generations and set the stage for transition rather than amputation or exodus. . . . This generation needs fathers and mothers in the faith, who love to hand off more than to hold on because they are able to enjoy success coming to someone other than themselves and because they love mission more than they love power. . . . Those receiving the baton will commit fully to the race if they see older people doing the same, with the goal of forming a partnership that expands everyone's potential. . . . [An emerging leader] must become someone's son in the faith today. An older leader must pray for him, love him, and involve him right now, passing the baton to him and his generation. No one else is coming.[25]

## Making it Personal

1.  Have you ever been in a place of leadership where you felt like you were the only one left?

2.  Why do most of us find it difficult to share our lives with fellow believers and colleagues in a spirit of authenticity and genuine transparency?

3.  Have you ever been part of Christian community where genuine fellowship was readily available and faithfully practiced? What made it work?

4.  By God's grace, what practical steps can you take today to strengthen your spiritual friendships and deepen your participation in Christian community?

# Conclusion
## Taking off the Mask

*The angel of the Lord said to Elijah, "Go down with him; do not be afraid."* (2 Kings 1:15)

"I'm drowning." The moment I uttered those words on that cold, cloudy, January afternoon so many years ago, three things happened. First, I broke down and began to sob uncontrollably, which was highly unusual for me and more than a little scary yet extremely liberating at the same time. Second, I felt an unmistakable assurance of God's presence in the room—holding me, loving me, and grieving with me in much the same way I had sought to grieve with people in my congregation when they experienced a great loss. Third, I clearly heard a still, small voice whisper into my ear, "I love you, David, and I will never let you go." My circumstances did not change dramatically that day, but my life did.

A couple of months later one of my sisters happened to be in town. She also just happens to be a pastor. When I described what I had been going through, she looked at me and said rather matter-of-factly, "David, you're depressed." With shock on my face, I thought to myself, "I can't be depressed—I'm a pastor!" (How's that for spiritual heroism!) My sister went on to describe her own battle with depression and her growing realization that this is a common theme in our family history.

I'm not sure how I responded to her that day, but looking back on this experience (which took place during my fifteenth year in public ministry) I soon came to realize that my sister was right. I was depressed, and it wasn't the first time. With that realization came a growing gratitude for my sister's willingness to speak the truth in love that day, because that truth continues to set me free.

Several years later, as I read through the pages of *Coping with Depression in the Ministry* by Archibald Hart, my thoughts returned to that conversation with my sister during the winter of 1997. If I had read this book before, I think I would have read it solely as a means to help others deal with depression. I'm thankful I was able to read it on this side of that conversation because I have come to realize that my personal experience with depression has become one of my greatest resources for meaningful ministry. By the grace of God, I am gradually learning that some of the greatest blessings in life come through our deepest brokenness.

I have also come to believe that the greater our self-understanding, the greater our potential for understanding and helping others as they seek to grow in their relationship with God and with his people. This reality was recently reinforced by a colleague who shared the following quotation from a young, homeless man he had befriended: "When you are most in touch with your own pain," he offered, "it's there that you'll know mine." As Henri Nouwen would remind us, we are all "wounded healers," after all.

One of the most helpful sections in Hart's book is his treatment of the "Masking of Depression." As I reflected on his words, I began to think back on many of the sad days I experienced as a child, teenager, and young adult. As I connected the dots, I began to understand in new ways the pattern of depression that has been evident in my life and how I have attempted to mask it along the way.

On that cold, cloudy day in January 1997, I could hold up the facade no longer. The mask fell off. Through the timely insight of an older, wiser, and truly loving sister, I was empowered to recognize some of the reasons I had worn it in the first place. With the help of the Lord and the many caring people he has put in my life, I am hoping to keep it off for good.

Like Bruce Wayne in the final scene of *The Dark Knight Rises*, all who have been called to serve as spiritual leaders in the body of Christ must be willing to take off the masks that perpetuate the self-defeating facade of spiritual heroism. We must be willing to embrace the gift of limits and repent of our propensity for attempting to play God in order to avoid the painful realities that accompany our frail, fallen, finite, human existence. We must be willing to die to our false, meticulously manufactured alter-egos if we hope to rise and walk as our true selves, warts and all. And we can do so, secure in the knowledge that each of us is passionately, relentlessly and permanently loved by our good and gracious God.

He is the Lord God Almighty, after all, the Maker of heaven and earth. He is the God of Abraham, Isaac, and Jacob, not to mention Elijah and every other flawed yet faithful man and woman of God who has ever walked the face of this earth. He is the God and Father of our Lord Jesus Christ, and he is the lover of our souls. God is the only one qualified for the job, and he has no plans to retire.

If we are willing to take off our masks and let God be God, if we are willing to let him be our one and only hero, then we will have an opportunity to experience the truly good and beautiful life that God has planned for us, a life that is increasingly free from the life-threatening burdens of exhaustion, disillusionment, and isolation; and increasingly full of the life-giving benefits of physical refreshment, spiritual renewal, and vocational realignment. Over time and through the Lord's tender mercy, we will find that the yoke of spiritual leadership we have been called to share with Christ is not as heavy as it used to be. This lighter, gentler yoke is a much better fit than the old one. Our lives and ministries, while not immune from the normal pains and pressures of this world, somehow become more restful, more joyful, and much more sustainable. And if we listen closely, we may very well hear a still, small voice whisper gently into our ears:

"Welcome to the unforced rhythms of grace."

## Making it Personal

1. What masks are you most tempted to wear as a means of perpetuating the self-defeating façade of spiritual heroism?

2. By God's grace, what steps can you take today to begin removing these masks and enter more fully into our Lord's unforced rhythms of grace?

# Appendix
## Creating Your Own Rhythm of Life

*Adapted by David Williams, from an article written by Demi Prentiss, a member of St. Mark's Episcopal Church, San Antonio, TX

You are not creating the Rhythm of Life for all people or for all time (Jesus has already taken care of that). You are not creating a rhythm for your entire life (it's not meant to account for every minute, eliminate spontaneity, or remain unchanged until death). You are cocreating your own rhythm of life, in conversation with the lover of your soul, the One who made you in his very own image and who knows you much better than you know yourself. You are committing to begin a practice that, with the Lord's help, will remove some of the obstacles that may hinder you on your journey with Jesus.

Be gentle with yourself. Remember that you are a precious, beloved child of God right now, just as you are. And God wants a deeper relationship with you (yes, you!). Don't create a legalistic straitjacket for yourself. This is not a competition. It isn't an event for spiritual superheroes. And don't let yourself be such a softie that you never find the edges of your comfort zone. As Dallas Willard would remind us, "Grace is opposed to earning, not effort."

The very first step to creating a rhythm of life is to take stock of where you already are. Once that's clear, it's easier to give attention to the things that truly matter and to make time for the things that are most important to you.

So take a piece of paper. Draw a vertical line that divides the paper in half. Then, about two-thirds of the way down the page, draw a horizontal line. Label the top two quadrants "daily" and "weekly." Label the bottom (smaller) quadrants "monthly" (or "quarterly") and "yearly."

In each of these quadrants, write down whatever you already do on purpose that helps you become more mindful of God at work in your life, whether daily, weekly, monthly, quarterly, or yearly. Daily quiet time or reading, weekly participation in corporate worship or Bible study, a monthly meeting, or an annual retreat are examples of what you might write down. But you might also include serving at a soup kitchen, or making music, or managing an on-line prayer list, or crusading for affordable housing, or saying, "Lord have mercy," instead of losing your temper.

Be honest. This is not a test of your piety (no one's looking over your shoulder), and it is not a wish list of what you hope to do someday. If there's only one thing (or nothing!), that's a fine place to start. If you already have lots of things crowding the spaces, one of your challenges may be to prune some of your activities.

You might think of your rhythm of life as a personal GPS system. Next to each item on your list, write a "G" if it emphasizes cultivating your personal relationship with God (prayer, journaling, etc.). Write a "P" if it focuses on building relationships with other people, both Christians and non-Christians (small groups, personal evangelism, etc.). Write an "S" if it represents an area of self-care (exercise, rest, etc.). This rhythm of life is grounded in Jesus' Great Commandment:

> Love the Lord your *God* with all your heart and with all your soul and with all your mind and with all your strength, . . . [and] love your *neighbor* as *yourself* (Mark 12:30-31, emphasis mine).

Now, prayerfully, and perhaps over an extended period of time, examine how God might be calling you to revise your current practice. Consider several questions:

- Is my present practice right for today, truly reflecting who I am, or is it something arrived at by accident, or as a leftover from another time in my life?
- Does my present practice reflect balance among the four quadrants, and among the God, people, and self components?
- Is the rhythm right for me?
- Does some element appear to be missing or underdeveloped?
- How might God be calling me to adjust my present practice by adding one or two items, or by taking something away, or by changing frequency in order to deepen my relationship with my Creator?

Write down your rhythm of life as God has led you to understand it. Include your daily, weekly, monthly, and yearly practices. Offer it to God as a covenant. Post it in a place where it will speak to you but not where you'll become blind to it due to overexposure.

As you feel led to make a change in your practice, be sure to move into it gently. Be careful to test each change for a time, so you can determine if the new practice is a fruitful one. Remember that the object of the exercise is to deepen your relationship with God. Review how well you are practicing your rhythm of life regularly. Enlist the help of a trusted community of friends or a spiritual director to help you both perceive the Christ pattern in your life and understand how you are living into it.

Revisit your rhythm of life once a year (on your birthday, perhaps) to discern whether it still fits you. Revise it as needed, using the same process you used to write it.

# Notes

## Introduction

1.  Richard J. Krejcir, "Francis Schaeffer Statistics
    on Pastors," Schaeffer Institute, 2007, accessed
    July 11, 2012, http://www.intothyword.org/
    apps/articles/default.asp?articleid=36562&-
    columnid=3958. Krejcir's summary of clergy
    health (and disease) was constructed from var-
    ious snapshots that have been collected over
    the past fifteen years or so. The general pat-
    terns that emerge have not changed significantly
    since similar results were initially reported
    in a study conducted by Fuller Theological
    Seminary in 1995. This disturbing profile of
    clergy health has been repeatedly corrobo-
    rated by subsequent studies in more recent
    years as well. A survey conducted by LifeWay
    Research in 2010, for example, found that al-
    most all pastors feel privileged to be in ministry,
    but a majority also feel lonely and discouraged
    (see David Roach, "Pastors Feel Privileged and
    Positive, Though Discouragement Can Come,"
    LifeWay, (October 5, 2011), www.lifeway.com/

Research-Survey-Pastors-feel-privileged-and-positive-though-discouragement-can-come.

2. Ted Haggard, "Letter to New Life Church Family" (letter presented to New Life Church, Colorado Springs, CO, November 5, 2006).

3. *Merriam-Webster OnLine*, s.v. "burnout," accessed October 28, 2008, http://www.merriam-webster.com/dictionary/burnout.

4. David P. Mann, "Preventing Burnout in Ministry: A Health and Wellness Approach," *Ashland Theological Journal* (2007): 49.

5. Sheri S. Ferguson, "Clergy Compassion Fatigue," *Family Therapy* (March-April 2007): 16.

6. Bob Wells, "Which Way to Clergy Health?," *Divinity,* (Fall 2002): 4-9, pdf accessed October 29, 2008, http://www.divinity. duke.edu/docs/ Magazine/DivmagFall2002.

7. Dean R. Hoge and Jacqueline E. Wenger, "Experiences of Protestant Ministers Who Left Local Church Ministry" (presented to the Religious Research Association, Norfolk, VA, October 25, 2003). According to the authors, "The best data comes from the Evangelical Lutheran Church in America, where 15% of the newly ordained in 1988 left the roster of clergy (which includes both local church ministers and specialized ministers) in the subsequent thirteen years. The percentage leaving local church ministry was probably higher."

8. Ibid., 15.

9. Charles J. Conniry, Jr., *Soaring in the Spirit: Rediscovering Mystery in the Christian Life* (Tyrone, GA: Paternoster, 2007), 25-26, 34.

10. This pastor's story is used with his gracious permission, but for obvious reasons, any references to specific names, places, and dates have been withheld in order to safeguard his identity.

11. H. Norman Wright, *The New Guide to Crisis and Trauma Counseling* (Ventura, CA: Regal, 2003), 131.

12. Donald R. Hands and Wayne L. Fehr, *Spiritual Wholeness for Clergy: A New Psychology of Intimacy with God, Self, and Others* (Bethesda, MD: Alban Institute, 1993), 9.

13. Henri J. M. Nouwen, *In the Name of Jesus: Reflections on Christian Leadership* (New York: Crossroad, 1989), 53-54.

14. Sally Morgenthaler, "Does Ministry Fuel Addictive Behavior?," *Leadership* (Winter 2006): 61. Our female colleagues seem to have an unusually clear understanding of these issues. Like Morgenthaler, author Susan Howatch has illustrated well the perils of spiritual heroism and image management in a series of six insightful novels based on the Church of England. Titles include *Glittering Images, Glamorous Powers,* and *Ultimate Prizes.*

15. Gene Edwards's book *A Tale of Three Kings* (Tyndale, 1992) provides tremendous insight into the relationship between blessing and brokenness in the lives of spiritual leaders.

16. Peter Scazzero, and Warren Bird, *The Emotionally Healthy Church: A Strategy for Discipleship That Actually Changes Lives* (Grand Rapids: Zondervan, 2003), 136-46.

17. Special thanks to David Nixon for contributing this term to my ministry vocabulary. See Dave's website for more information: http://www.sustainablefaith.com.

18. Special thanks to Eugene Peterson for including this delightful phrase in his translation of Matthew 11:29 in *The Message*. As should be obvious by now, this is the very phrase that inspired the title for this book.

## Chapter One: The Rhythm of Physical Refreshment

1. Curt Thompson, *Anatomy of the Soul: Surprising Connections between Neuroscience and Spiritual Practices That Can Transform Your Life and Relationships* (Carol Stream, IL: Tyndale, 2010), 29.

2. The Greek word most commonly used in the New Testament to describe a "change in thinking" is *metanoia*, i.e. repentance.

3. Stefanie Paulsell, *Honoring the Body: Meditations on a Christian Practice* (San Francisco: Jossey-Bass, 2002), quoted in Wells, "Which Way," 2-5.

4. Hands and Fehr, *Spiritual Wholeness*, 75-76.

5. Wells, "Which Way," 3.

6. Archibald D. Hart, *Adrenalin and Stress* (Dallas: Word, 1991), 145-51.

7. Ibid., 88-89.

8. G. Lloyd Rediger, *Clergy Killers: Guidance for Pastors and Congregations under Attack* (Louisville: Westminster John Knox Press, 1997), 164.

9. For an excellent treatment of this topic, see Dennis Okholm, "Rx for Gluttony," *Christianity Today* (September 4, 2000). For additional context, see Grant Martin, *When Good Things Become Addictions* (Wheaton: Victor, 1990).

10. Paulsell, *Honoring the Body*, quoted in Wells, "*Which Way,*" 4.

11. Ibid., 145.

12. The Barna Group, "Americans Just Want A Good Night of Sleep," *The Barna Update* (October 16, 2006), accessed October 31, 2008 http://www.barna.org/FlexPage.aspx?Page=BarnaUpdate&BarnaUpdateID=247.

13. Hart, Adrenalin and Stress, 22.

14. Thanks again to David Nixon for providing these practical tips on developing healthy sleep patterns.

15. H. B. London, Jr. and Neil B. Wiseman, *Pastors at Greater Risk: Real Help for Pastors from Pastors Who've Been There* (Ventura, CA: Regal, 2003), 172. As the former vice president of ministry outreach/pastoral ministries for *Focus on the Family*, London is uniquely qualified to assess the concerns of pastors and their families based on over fifty years of personal experience and regular contact with thousands of pastors from across the country.

16. Samuel D. Rima, *Leading from the Inside Out: The Art of Self-Leadership* (Grand Rapids: Baker, 2000), 29-30. For those who are interested in exploring the topic of self-leadership further, Rima has a website (www.samrima.com), which provides additional resources based on this book and its predecessor, *Overcoming the Dark Side of Leadership* (Grand Rapids: Baker, 1997), co-written with Gary McIntosh. For a nominal fee, Rima promises to "coach you in complet- ing the on-line, interactive workshops and assist you in developing your Personal Constitution, Self-leadership Plan, as well as your Dark Side Profile and a Personal Plan to manage your dark side so that it doesn't mitigate your leadership. Then, [he] will help hold you accountable to liv- ing out your self-leadership plans and coach you through the initial obstacles you will face." This author has found such resources to be of great benefit in the development of an ongoing plan for personal fitness, discipleship, and spiritual formation.

## Chapter Two: The Rhythm of Spiritual Renewal

1. It has been a custom of mine for many years now to read this passage before setting out on a hiking, backpacking, or mountain climbing ad- venture, whether on my own or with a group of friends. In my Bible, a handwritten heading has been inserted just above Psalm 121: "The Backpacker's Psalm."

2. Tom Gill, ed., *The Confessions of Saint Augustine* (Gainesville, FL: Bridge-Logos, 2004), 1.

3. This is the chorus from "In the Garden" ("I Come to the Garden Alone") by C. Austin Miles.

4. Thomas R. Kelly, *A Testament of Devotion* (New York: HarperCollins, 1941), 89-90.

5. "Digital Set to Surpass TV in Time Spent with US Media," *eMarketer*, (August 1, 2013), accessed June 19, 2014, http://www.emarketer.com/Article/Digital-Set-Surpass-TV-Time-Spent-with-US-Media/1010096#sthash.jzRdSOTH.dpuf.

6. "Digital Set," *eMarketer*, August 1, 2013.

7. Kelly, *Testament of Devotion*, 92.

8. Ibid., 118, 120. See also T. Canby Jones, *Thomas Kelly as I Remember Him* (Wallingford, PA: Pendle Hill, 1988), 25-31. According to Jones, a friend and student of Kelly, this "cataclysmic event" was preceded by a series of devastating disappointments, which were accompanied by seasons of depression, suicidal thoughts, and a complete nervous breakdown. Special thanks to my friend Richard Sartwell for bringing this to my attention.

9. Ibid., 100.

10. Sigve Tonstad, "The Limits of Power: Revisiting Elijah and Horeb," *SJOT* 19, no. 2 (2005): 256.

11. Ibid.

12. Fil Anderson, *Running on Empty: Contemplative Spirituality for Overachievers* (Colorado Springs: WaterBrook Press, 2004), 1-6.

13. *Merriam-Webster OnLine Dictionary*, s.v. "disillusion," accessed November 19, 2008, http://www.merriam-webster.com/dictionary/sustain.

14. Peter Scazzero, *Emotionally Healthy Spirituality* (Nashville: Thomas Nelson, 2006), 117-33.

15. Brennan Manning, *The Ragamuffin Gospel: Embracing the Unconditional Love of God* (Sisters, OR: Multnomah, 1990), 199.

16. See Richard Foster's *Life with God* (San Francisco: HarperOne, 2008) for a thorough treatment of the call to embrace the "with-God-life" that permeates not only the Gospels, but the whole of Scripture.

17. Scazzero, *Emotionally Healthy Spirituality*, 131.

18. Richard J. Foster, *Celebration of Discipline: The Path to Spiritual Growth*, 20th Anniversary ed. (San Francisco: HarperCollins, 1998), 1.

19. Gordon MacDonald, *Ordering Your Private World* (Nashville: Nelson, 1984), 29-30.

20. Anderson, *Running on Empty*, 3-4.

21. Special thanks to Eugene Peterson, Henri Nouwen and Dan Brunner for each of their contributions to the concepts described in this section. The diagram itself is taken directly from the class notes for DMIN 512 Spiritual Formation and the Minister (George Fox Evangelical Seminary, October 11, 2006) and is used with the gracious permission of Brunner.

22. Eugene Peterson, "The Pastor's Sabbath," *Leadership* 6, no. 1 (Spring 1985): 55-56.

23. MacDonald, *Ordering Your Private World*, 13.

24. Ibid., 172.

25. Shelton Smith, "G. Campbell Morgan," (Sword of the Lord Publishers, 2008), accessed December 16, 2008, http://www.swordofthe-lord.com/biographies/MorganGCampbell.htm.

26. Patrick J. Johnstone, Robyn J. Johnstone, and Jason Mandryk, *Operation World*, 21st Century ed. (Waynesboro, GA: Paternoster, 2001), 387-88.

27. Dallas Willard, *In Search of Guidance: Developing a Conversational Relationship with God* (Ventura, CA: Regal, 1984), 33.

28. Richard Rohr, *Everything Belongs: The Gift of Contemplative Prayer*, rev. ed. (New York: Crossroad, 2003), 67.

29. Special thanks to Fil Anderson, executive director of Journey Resources, for his profound influence upon my understanding and practice of prayer. You can find much more valuable assistance in this area on his website: www.journey-resources.com.

30. The term *rule of life* refers to "a preferred pattern for the personal and/or communal practice of Christian life and ministry." It was made popular by Benedict of Nursa (c. 480-547), and was formally articulated in a monastic manual that eventually became known as *The Rule of St. Benedict*, one of the most influential documents in Western Christendom. Benedict's *Rule* is heavily influenced by the Desert Fathers, especially John Cassian.

31. Os Guinness, *The Call: Finding and Fulfilling the Central Purpose of Your Life* (Nashville: Thomas Nelson, 2003), 70-72.

## Chapter Three: The Rhythm of Vocational Realignment

1. Manning, *Ragamuffin Gospel*, 132.

2. Dietrich Bonhoeffer, *Life Together* (New York: Harper, 1954), 23.

3. Henri J. M. Nouwen, Donald P. McNeill and Douglas A. Morrison, *Compassion: A Reflection on the Christian Life* (London: Darton, Longman and Todd, 1982), 121-22.

4. Ibid., 60.

5. Robert Jamieson and A. R. Fausset, *A Commentary, Critical and Explanatory, on the Old and New Testaments*. 1 Kings 17:1. (Oak Harbor, WA: Logos Research Systems, Inc., 1997).

6. George Gallup, Jr., *The People's Religion* (New York: Macmillan, 1989), quoted in Joseph Myers, *The Search to Belong* (Grand Rapids: Zondervan, 2003), 23.

7. Miller McPherson, Lynn Smith-Lovin, and Matthew E. Brashears, "Social Isolation in America: Changes in Core Discussion Networks over Two Decades," *American Sociological Review* 71 (June 2006): 353-75.

8. Thompson, *Anatomy of the Soul*, 3.

9. Hands and Fehr, *Spiritual Wholeness*, xx.

10. Ibid., 25.

11. William N. Grosch and David C. Olsen, "Clergy Burnout: An Integrative Approach," *Journal of Clinical Psychology* 56, no. 5 (2000): 624-25.

12. Ibid., 8-14.

13. Ibid., 579.

14. Ferguson, "Clergy Compassion Fatigue," 18.

15. Scott M. Peck, *The Different Drum: Community Making and Peace* (New York: Simon and Schuster, 1987), 58.

16. Ibid., 31.

17. Bonhoeffer, *Life Together*, 112-13.

18. Gerald G. May, *Addiction and Grace* (San Francisco: Harper & Row, 1988), 45-46.

19. Archibald D. Hart, *Coping with Depression in the Ministry and Other Helping Professions* (Waco: Word, 1984), 17-18.

20. Nowhere is this more beautifully portrayed than in the icon of the Holy Trinity by Andrei Rublev, based on Abraham's encounter with the three visitors as recorded in Genesis 18:1-15.

21. Joseph R. Myers, *The Search to Belong: Rethinking Intimacy, Community, and Small Groups* (Grand Rapids: Zondervan, 2003), 20.

22. See Joseph R. Myers, *Organic Community: Creating a Place Where People Naturally Connect* (Grand Rapids: Baker, 2007), 133-43. According to Myers, "An editor's function is very different from that of an accountant. While an accountant's training, job, and passion are rooted in looking for errors and covering all bases, an

editor's training, job, and passion are to help an author toward richer communication—a rich, full voice that is free of encumbrances. Accountants keep records. Editors wipe away errors while keeping the voice of the author."

23. Jamieson and Fausset, *A Commentary*, 1 Kings 2:9.

24. Earl Creps, *Off-Road Disciplines: Spiritual Adventures for Missional Leaders* (San Francisco: Jossey-Bass, 2006), 51.

25. Ibid., 175-84.

CPSIA information can be obtained
at www.ICGtesting.com
Printed in the USA
FFOW03n2133251117
43674590-42493FF

9 781594 980404